TOURNAMENT TOUGH

TOURNAMENT TOUGH

CARLOS GOFFI

With Commentaries by John McEnroe

Edited by William Davies ▪ Chapters by Mary Carillo and Dr. Irving Glick
Additional Commentaries by Peter Fleming and Patrick McEnroe

HOLT, RINEHART AND WINSTON   NEW YORK

First published in January 1985 by Holt, Rinehart and Winston,
383 Madison Avenue, New York, New York 10017.
Published simultaneously in Canada by Holt, Rinehart
and Winston of Canada, Limited.

Library of Congress Cataloging in Publication Data
Goffi, Carlos.
Tournament tough.
1. Tennis—Training.   I. McEnroe,John, 1959–   II. Title.
GV1002.9.T7G64   1984   796.342'2   84-19741
ISBN 0-03-071598-9

First Edition

Designed by Susan Hood
Printed in the United States of America
1 2 3 4 5 6 7 8 9 10

ISBN 0-03-071598-9

To Jordan, Josh, and all the other junior
players around the world

CONTENTS

PREFACE

Having dedicated most of my life to tennis (from my earliest years as a junior on through college, and as a professional) and reflecting on all the varied experiences during my coaching career, I take pleasure in sharing with you the concepts I feel are important in developing a junior tennis player to his full potential.

Although in this book I discuss the importance of technical and physical development, its main objective is to address and unlock the unlimited potential in each one of us. Only by putting that potential to work can one attain maximum performance during competitive tennis.

Many juniors, including very young ones, as well as their parents, coaches, and senior players, have questions about the "behind the scenes" aspects of the game. *Tournament Tough* is intended to provide clear and simple answers to these questions. I've included some analogies and generalities in order to help translate these somewhat complex psychological issues.

Literary conventions may make it appear that the text is specifically meant for the male player. Obviously, it is not. As Mary Carillo puts it so well, "It would be archaic in this day and age to think female players shouldn't train as males do."

I am grateful to my dear friends for their contributions to this work: Mary Carillo, Peter Fleming, Dr. Irving Glick, and Patrick and John McEnroe. I am also grateful to another close friend, William Davies, who helped in editing my original manuscript, and Richard Seaver for his final touch.

Finally, I must acknowledge a special debt of appreciation to my parents for their support during my tennis career, and to Jeanne for having shared with me the entire process of publishing *Tournament Tough*.

I sincerely hope that you enjoy this book and that it may serve its purpose: a contribution to the enrichment of junior tennis.

Carlos Goffi, John McEnroe, and Peter Fleming at the Mutual Benefit Life Open, 1977

Edward Friedman

TOURNAMENT TOUGH

1 *YOUR CHAMPIONSHIP POTENTIAL*

Beppe Merlo could not play tennis. I kept on waiting for him to stop playing with the crowd and hit a huge topspin backhand or a vicious serve. But he did not. He just kept on puffing and wheezing, pushing back little chipped backhands, gasping under his breath to some invisible companion that he was getting too old and would probably have to stop before the end of the set. His steel racket, a battle-scarred club that looked for all the world as though it came from some ancient mail-order catalogue, trailed along the red clay court between each exhausting point and the next.

I was twenty then and had been chosen as player-captain of Brazil's squad for the Galea Cup (the international under-twenty-one team event), which was being held that year in Switzerland. I had arrived early and was playing the Geneva leg of the country's summer circuit to get acclimated. And I could not believe my eyes. Here was a forty-six-year-old Italian, with absolutely no serve, no evidence of a volley, and not a winning groundstroke to his name, soundly beating a talented top-ranked player. I stared at his backhand again as he scraped back another ball, his reversed two-handed grip choking up on the racket as if he were some rank beginner, scarcely visible through the cloud of clay kicked up by the tangled confusion of red-soiled tennis shoes that constituted his footwork.

Yet Beppe won not only that match, but several others as well. Furthermore, he had reached the finals of the Italian Open twice, the semi's of the French twice, had represented Italy more than forty times in the Davis Cup and had beaten a stream of Wimbledon champions from Don Budge and Jaraslav Drobny to Barry McKay and Chuck McKinley. How on earth could he do it?

I had spent my entire playing career working on my strokes, improving my fitness, building up my game physically and technically, yet here was a player who seemed to have little or no apparent physical or technical ability who could not only beat many

Merlo's unorthodox style

World Tennis

players who were less than half his age but had also beaten some of the greatest names in the game.

That match taught me what I hope this book will teach you: namely, that being successful at tennis is finally not about having the hardest serve or the best topspin backhand, any more than a clear complexion and film-star good looks are what ultimately determine your success with the opposite sex. Success in tennis, as

Notice Merlo's reversed grip.

World Tennis

in everything else, is about believing in yourself, in your ability to overcome any challenge. A number of top players have backhands as sharp, and volleys as punishing, as John McEnroe's, but he is still number one in the world, essentially and primarily because of his competitive attitude. He is tournament tough, just as Beppe Merlo was.

Coaches and commentators talk about the mental aspect of the game, and you will have heard and read a hundred times that tennis is 70 percent mental and only 30 percent technical and physical. Yet 90 percent of all coaching concentrates almost exclusively on the shots.

One of the oldest myths in the game is that mental toughness, tournament toughness, is something with which you are born: either you have it or you don't. This is simply not true. Just as anyone can learn to hit a backhand if he really wants to and learn to get a respectable score at Pacman if he really wants to, anyone can learn to believe in himself, learn to be more determined, learn to concentrate better. Some people are born with a head start in some areas—one kid can run faster, one kid can read better, one kid is more confident—but they can all improve their own skills in each area and even out the differences. Imagine that we were all born stereo sets; some of us have the volume on 3 when we arrive, and some of us have it on 7, but anyone can crank the tunes if he wants; he just has to turn himself up, to let it all out. The potential is there in everyone. The junior's first task is to understand this simple fact: that he can be as tough a player as he lets himself be. All the ability is in him; it is up to him to channel it. So get psyched, and whether you want to be the best player in your school, your city, or the world, start believing that if you want it badly enough, you have a good chance of getting it.

Now we can start going places.

Your championship potential

Michael Cole

Reminders

- Success in tennis, as in everything else, is about believing in yourself, in your ability to overcome any challenge.
- Just as anyone can learn to hit a backhand if he really wants to and learn to get a respectable score at Pacman if he really wants to, anyone can learn to believe in himself, learn to be more determined, learn to concentrate better.

John McEnroe's Commentary

There really isn't one particular moment, as far as I can remember, when I realized that tennis was largely a mental game. I didn't analyze it like that. I was always competitive, even before winning my first tournament (the club 12-and-under when I was eight).

But there's no doubt that being competitive, and being mentally tough enough to overcome any challenge, is one of the tennis player's most important weapons. It can take you a lot further than a big forehand can. It is also a never-ending learning process. The challenges I had to overcome during my junior career keep reappearing in the pros.

There are thousands of people playing tennis for a living, but only 128 of them get into Wimbledon or the U.S. Open. Just walk around the outside courts during the first days of either of these tournaments. These players are there not necessarily because they are fitter, stronger, or even more talented. There are scores of players who can hit every shot in the book who never make it into a Grand Slam event. These 128 are there because they are mentally tougher: they *wanted* it more. I can remember kids whom I played in the juniors who won just about everything and then didn't even try to make it. Physical and technical differences can count for a lot when you're twelve, but in the pros the game is much more a mental battle. The toughest guys win, not the biggest or the most coordinated.

2 TOURNAMENT TOUGH

The first step in becoming tournament tough is understanding exactly what the term means. Tournament toughness is that mental resilience and flexibility that separate champions from the pack, allowing them to win against opponents who are technically more skillful and physically more powerful, even when they are playing poorly themselves.

In some people these qualities are from birth more fully developed than in others. John McEnroe is a perfect example of this. When he was one of the juniors I was teaching at the Port Washington Tennis Academy in New York, I could never understand why he would lose interest in the practice drills I set up. It wasn't until I watched him playing a match and saw how every ounce of his mental, as well as his physical, energy was being channeled into winning that I realized just how mature a player he already was. Learning technique and practicing shots had become boring for him, not because he could already do anything he wanted with the ball, but because he had somehow already realized that a player is not as good as his shots. Shots come and go, but if you have the right competitive attitude, you can win.

Most fifteen-year-olds do not have that mental maturity, however, and still need a great deal of work on their games. My program does not cut out technical instruction entirely but blends it with mental instruction, the balance being determined by the age of the child. There are three distinct phases in a junior's career, each with its own mix of technical, physical, and mental development, building up to a game that is 70 percent mental and 30 percent technical and physical. For the ten-year-old beginner, however, the percentages will probably be 70 percent technical and only 30 percent mental and physical, perhaps even less, but as he grows older, the emphasis will shift from the physical and technical to the mental side of the game.

The three phases can be roughly divided as follows: ten to thirteen years old, thirteen to fifteen years old, and fifteen to eighteen years old. The most important phase by far is the middle one, ages thirteen to fifteen. In the initial phase, the very young junior is largely acquiring a "feel" for the ball and beginning to gain some tournament experience, whereas in the final one he may well be playing adult or even pro events, with his junior status a mere technicality (for example, Tracy Austin, Carling Bassett, Jimmy Arias, Kathy Rinaldi, Bjorn Borg). The middle phase is when the real work must be done, but it is also the time when the junior is dealing with all the problems and confusions of puberty.

By the time the ambitious junior has reached the age of thirteen, he will have begun to understand how important the game is to him and will have some tournament experience behind him. Until now the emphasis will have been very much on learning "the shots" and making the game fun. Now is the time to shift it more toward the mental side—while making sure that the game is still fun.

However simplistic it may seem, it is important to understand that any tennis match begins fairly evenly balanced; each player has about a 50-percent chance of winning. Anything you can do to alter that balance in your favor will help you to win, whether it's having a better serve, a more effective baseline game, or a stronger mental attitude. When Harold Solomon was active on the tour, the odds were most of the time heavily stacked against

Easter Bowl Champion—McEnroe during his 7–6, 6–4 upset victory over Larry Gottfried in the Boys' 14.

World Tennis

him in physical and technical terms. Yet Solomon remained in the top ten for many years largely because he learned to tip the balance in his favor by acquiring a stronger mental attitude, which often neutralized his opponent's technical and physical advantages.

What does this attitude consist of? "Tournament toughness" consists of three distinct parts: self-confidence, determination, and concentration.

Each of these areas can be built up by using different drills and practices. The first step, and the key to the whole process, is clarifying and understanding your goals, which has the effect of developing both your concentration and your determination.

One of the great natural gifts that young people possess is their ability to dream, and, properly handled, this can be turned to

Fleming's trademark—his determination

Michael Cole

Tournament tough

Michael Cole

their advantage as tennis players. Rather than simply dreaming in vivid Technicolor of one day becoming Wimbledon champion and imagining yourself holding the trophy above your head, you must split that dream into a series of smaller dreams, each leading to the next. In other words, you draw up an ultimate dream, an intermediate dream, and an immediate dream, making each a distinct goal.

Let's shoot for the moon and say your ultimate goal is playing at the U.S. Open (though it could be playing at the National 14s or winning your city championships). Your intermediate goal should then be to gain a national ranking in the top thirty of your age group by the time you are sixteen. Your immediate goal would then be winning the state championship in your division this summer. By dividing up your goals, building a path of steppingstones to your ultimate goal, you make it closer and more attainable, and this means you can channel your energy more efficiently.

At the same time, understand that being the winner means simply being *better* than your opponents in the field. A lot of kids psych themselves out of winning because they get caught up striving for perfection. They spend hours on the practice court trying to develop a *perfect* backhand or a *perfect* toss on their serve, when all they need is a game that is well rounded, and good enough to beat whoever is on the other side of the net. When John McEnroe and Jimmy Connors win Wimbledon and the U.S. Open, people shake their heads in amazement as if they're magic or just cruise through the draw, winning every round love and love. They don't. There are times when they're out there in the early rounds barely scraping through in the fifth set, playing just well enough to win. They know that every shot isn't going to be perfect, but they're always striving to make them at least good enough to win the match. Remember Beppe Merlo!

Visualize yourself being successful before playing matches, or before taking exams, and again make it practical. Don't just dream about being number one in the nation or the state, or getting straight As in school; think about what you have to do to achieve those goals and start doing it. Make these images a part of yourself so that you actually become the successful person you are visualizing. Start by dressing as "he" would, by coping with pressure as "he" would; always keep a clear picture of what you need to do to get where "he" is. Your self-confidence will grow, and as it does, success will become closer.

Explanation of the Three Phases of Junior Tennis

In the first phase of junior tennis, it is important to keep it fun. I recommend holding a really keen child back until he is ten or eleven, not letting him play many tournaments or receive intensive coaching from a pro before then, even if he is one of those special kids who cry out for it at seven or eight. If you let kids go wild that young, it's too easy for them to burn out. Holding them back keeps them hungry and fuels their motivation. Keeping the

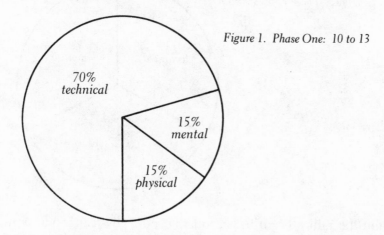

Figure 1. Phase One: 10 to 13

game fun at this stage means having the kids hit the ball over the net, time and time again, and play enjoyable games with family and friends. Also, it doesn't make sense to go overboard with physical training at this age; at ten or eleven the child is often growing fast, about to start his teen-age spurt, his body in a state of flux. If a child can come through this first stage hitting the ball fairly consistently and still be really hungry, the prospects for the future are good.

The second phase is by far the most important one. By the time they reach fifteen, many boys and girls are as tall as their parents; the boys are often hitting the ball as hard as better adult players and girls often play some women's and even pro events. A certain amount of work remains to be done on their technical game—often adapting or coordinating it to fit the sometimes drastic and rapid changes in their growth patterns. However, with an increasingly intensive tournament schedule during school vacations, much more attention is now paid to the mental aspects of the game, particularly in pacing matches and identifying big points. Also, as the youngsters get bigger, the ball starts to move faster

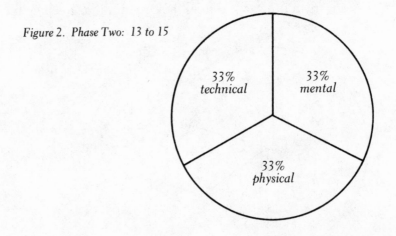

Figure 2. Phase Two: 13 to 15

33%
technical

33%
mental

33%
physical

and the rallies begin to get tougher; now physical conditioning becomes much more important. Great care must be taken during this phase, since it is at this point that demands on time, money, and emotion become more acute and player-parent relationships can begin to sour.

By the final year of phase three—that is, the age of eighteen—players are for the most part physically mature and should have become much tougher mentally from the experience of all the matches they have played. For many players on the tour this isn't so much the last phase of junior tennis as the first stage of pro tennis. The mental leap involved in no longer thinking of yourself as a junior but as a player capable of beating adults on the tour is a big one. So at this stage the emphasis must move more toward mental toughness. The proportion may still not have reached the ideal 70 percent mental versus 30 percent technical and physical, but it is getting close. During phase three, the junior player should be comfortable with his strokes and start to identify the strongest and most reliable weapons in his game that can be used to intimidate his opponents.

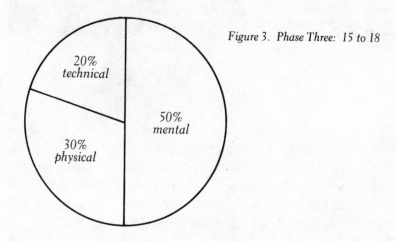

Figure 3. Phase Three: 15 to 18

What can hold back even the strongest kids who are coming out of the juniors onto the tour is lack of stamina. However fit you may be, the vastly greater competitive pressure of the pro tour takes much more out of your body than probably any match a junior may have played. A twenty-stroke rally in the first round of the French, in front of several thousand people, against a player in the top hundred, takes a lot more out of you than an equivalent rally even at the National 18s. In addition, the rising junior has probably had to play as many as six matches in qualifying and pre-qualifying rounds just to reach the main draw. So building stamina is a high priority at this stage of your tennis life.

Don't lose heart if you're seventeen and are not ranked in the top thirty in the country yet. There are no rules when it comes to making it; it's all a matter of how much you want it. I doubt very much whether Beppe Merlo paid much attention to rules about when and how to make it, and the fact that his wins did not come easily apparently did not bother him at all. It may even have helped.

Katherine Chabot, a 6–1, 8–6 winner over Billie Jean King (then Billie Jean Moffitt) in the finals of the Pacific-Southwest International Tennis Championships (girls' 15). Even Billie Jean had her troubles in the juniors.

Thelner Hoover

When a player is tournament tough his competitive attitude is always positive. Understanding that at the start of a match both he and his opponent are closely matched, the tournament-tough player sees his basic task as doing everything he can to tip the balance in his favor. If his opponent begins to push ahead, either technically (say, by getting a very high percentage of first serves in) or mentally (his confidence beginning to grow from a streak of points won), the tough player spots these shifts in balance early and, rather than panicking, regards them as a challenge to be overcome. He has confidence in his ability to meet any challenge, and simply sets about analyzing the changed balance, working out how he can re-establish it in his favor. In other words, his mental attitude is one of self-confidence and determination.

The other keystone of tournament toughness, being able to maintain concentration in a match, stems directly from a player's confidence and determination. If they are strong, he will remain alert to the constant shifting of the match's balance because he is in control. However, there are a number of other ways in which concentration can be built up. For instance, tennis players can develop their skills on video and computer games, which require not only long periods of deep concentration, but also razor-sharp hand-eye coordination. One widely observed myth about young players is that it makes no sense to try to teach them how to concentrate better, because at twelve or fourteen they simply don't have the capacity to focus their attention on a single subject for any length of time. Yet I remember watching one eleven-year-old, whom I had started in the game, playing Pacman. He had just beaten the highest score and was locked into a second game, applying many skills similar to those required in competitive tennis. And yet people still think that kids can't concentrate. Whether it's video games, soccer, backgammon, or tennis, children can get deeply and quickly involved.

It may sound old-fashioned to describe tennis as physical chess, but in many ways it is exactly that, and the junior who can acquire a taste for the board game rapidly learns how to concentrate better by visualizing and anticipating two or three moves ahead. Younger players often show no interest in chess initially, but if they are given access to a computer-game version, the interest often develops very quickly—it's just more fun playing against a silicon chip.

When you are actually on court, there are many ways to keep your mind focused on the match and a most effective and useful way, the Two Selves Technique, I'll describe in the next chapter. You'll hear players and coaches mention other methods—watching the seams of the ball or the arc it makes over the net—but if your mind is wandering so much from the psychological balance of the match that you continually need these drills to stay aware of the basics of competition, I suspect that your commitment isn't what it should be. Staying aware of your opponent's possibilities and outthinking him in every point, game, and set should be more than enough to focus your attention.

Parents have often asked me, after I've explained this, whether I'm not making the kids take the game too seriously, whether they're not going to stop having fun with all this introspection and plotting. It's a good point, and one that both the player and his parents must understand.

If you ask John McEnroe or Peter Fleming whether playing the game is still fun, he'll tell you, "Sure, it *has* to be fun to make it worth doing." Yet although the two of them have fun, it isn't the sort of fun you have when you go to Disney World. It's the sort of fun that springs from seeing through your opponent technically, physically, and mentally, understanding how he is playing, and then outmaneuvering him. For want of a better term, I think of it as "competitive fun." Some parents will say, understandably, that they are uncertain whether they want their kids to acquire a taste for that sort of "fun," but the fact is, they already have it: we're all born with the competitive drive, though to varying degrees. Besides, what gives this fun its flavor is the way a player handles it. You can be sure that Borg, one of the greatest gentlemen in the modern game, never felt apologetic about beating an opponent in his Wimbledon finals. He loved every minute of it, loved outthinking, outmaneuvering, and outplaying the player across the net, just as McEnroe, Fleming, and all the other pros do. What counts is the way they handle the situation, and Borg is a perfect example. Though he had great fun running an opponent all over the court, he didn't try to rub salt in the wounds after winning. That's what tennis is about.

Reminders

- Shots come and go, but if you have the right competitive attitude, you can win.
- However simplistic it may seem, it is important to understand that any tennis match begins fairly evenly balanced; each player has about a 50-percent chance of winning.
- "Tournament toughness" consists of three distinct parts: self-confidence, determination, and concentration.
- However fit you may be, the vastly greater competitive pressure of the pro tour takes much more out of your body than probably any match a junior may have played.
- Don't lose heart if you're seventeen and are not ranked in the top thirty in the country yet.
- Staying aware of your opponent's possibilities and outthinking him in every point, game, and set should be more than enough to focus your attention.

John McEnroe's Commentary

It's hard for me to describe exactly what mental toughness is. Actually, I'm not sure how much a young junior needs to know about it. Older kids certainly have to be aware of it, but when you're starting out, the game is primarily technical and physical. You're just trying to get the ball over the net and stay on court for an hour and a half. In the juniors, a couple of extra inches in height, along with a year's more tournament experience, can make a huge difference (if you're fourteen with an unlucky birthday, you could be playing a sixteen-year-old with a lucky birthday who has two years more playing experience than you). I can remember playing and losing to opponents when I was a junior because they were too strong and too big. They simply overpowered me. Guys like Walter Redondo, who beat me 6–2, 6–1 in the Nationals, used to look like giants to me in the juniors, but as we grew up and I got bigger and tougher, the physical and technical differences between us came to mean much less.

I strongly believe that it's a lot easier to be mentally tough when you've got your goals straight (maybe when you're first starting, there are more hopes than goals). I don't think there are many kids who have picked up a racket who haven't dreamed of one day becoming pros. You've got to work out whether or not these goals are realistic. I'm sure that most of the kids who play tournaments or who want to play the Nationals wouldn't choose to be remembered just as good juniors. They want to go further. But you have to know how far you want to go, you have to be able to pace yourself; otherwise, you can burn yourself out.

3 VERSATILITY

Though you must learn to be tournament tough, be careful not to confuse being a tough player with being an inflexible player. As I have pointed out, a champion is one who can win under any circumstances, whether the sun is in his eyes, whether there's a howling wind, or whether he is facing an opponent who is physically and technically stronger. He succeeds by adapting to the particular circumstances of each match, by analyzing the obstacles and then selecting the most effective way of overcoming them. In other words, by being versatile.

One of the most misleading pieces of phony bite-the-bullet wisdom that the junior player is ever likely to hear (and with the growing army of tennis pseudoexperts, he is likely to hear it a lot) is the admonishment to "play your own game, kid," usually accompanied by a manly slap on the back. The idea is that even if you lose love and love, it doesn't really matter, because you played your natural game and eventually it will become so good that you'll win rather than lose matches with it. Forget it. It's like telling a swimmer in the medley race to swim every lap freestyle (it's his natural stroke) because even though he'll be disqualified from the breaststroke, backstroke, and butterfly sections, he will do well and keep improving in the freestyle. Even the greatest players in the world have to adapt their games to each opponent and court surface. Borg would hit flatter strokes with shorter swings at Wimbledon to compensate for the quick-playing grass courts, Chris Evert Lloyd built up her serve and her net game to give her more options on faster surfaces, and even Connors will sometimes suddenly break up his power game on certain vital points.

Given that you must learn to be versatile, be careful not to make the mistake that many TV commentators seem to encourage their viewers to make: that is, to assume that versatility means just chipping, drop-shotting, and lobbing. First of all, versatility can be suddenly serve-and-volleying, just as much as breaking up the flow of the point with spins and dinks. In 1983, when McEnroe was in the depth of his losing streak against Ivan Lendl, he decided to set a new trend for their bouts. He abandoned the strategy of mixing up the pace and chose to launch a full frontal assault on the Czech. The new tactic kept Lendl from getting grooved on his powerful groundstrokes and simply overpowered him both in Philadelphia early in the year and at the World Championship Tennis finals in Dallas. Versatility is simply doing whatever is necessary to win, whether or not it seems logical or natural.

Yet it is also important to realize that the specific tactics a player selects—whether it is staying back or serve-and-volleying—are only the visible signs of the far more important psychological struggle in which the two players are locked. When I was fourteen, I can remember watching a Davis Cup match between Spain and Brazil in São Paulo. The opening singles was between Manuel Santana, a Wimbledon champion and one of the greatest players in the sixties game, and Edson Mandarino, a tenacious clay-court player who held the advantage of playing on his home court before a vast crowd of exuberant Latin Americans hysterically screaming their support. Though Santana was indisputably the better player in terms of record, as they began to warm up he could feel Mandarino begin to feed off the crowd's wild support, getting more and more psyched up. The Brazilian won the toss, and the crowd went haywire, screaming and yelling as if he had just hit an ace on match point. As Mandarino got his first serve into play and the point got under way, Santana knew that he had to do something to set the psychological balance of the match in his favor. They had both dug in on the baseline and traded about six or seven huge shots when Santana suddenly hit what appeared to be a trick shot, a backhand just burning up with backspin. We all watched in a daze, including Mandarino, as the ball dropped over the net and then, the vicious spin biting into the deep red clay, bounced straight back over the net onto Santana's side.

Although Mandarino went on to win the game, the Spaniard had achieved what he set out to do: to neutralize the home player's psychological advantage by being completely unpredictable. The point is that it was the mental unpredictability that counted, not winning the specific point. Even if he had missed that shot, the effect would have been almost the same. Santana had started making his opponent guess, kept him from getting into a mental groove.

There is a simple technique you can use that allows you to analyze the psychological balance of a match and quickly figure out what steps are needed to shift it in your favor. It is called the Two Selves Technique and involves, as you might have guessed, imagining that you are split into two people—one a TV commentator (a very good TV commentator) and the other a player. From the moment you walk onto the court, allow your TV-Commentator Self to start analyzing the court, the crowd, the weather conditions, and then your opponent beginning to warm up, just as the network pundits do. Let the Commentator tell the Player Self what to do at each point, which way the mental balance is shifting, what to do to alter it or neutralize the opponent's moves. If this does nothing else, it keeps you alert during the match, for just like the real TV commentators, the Commentator must absorb everything going on on the court. Not just the ball, but the score, the weather conditions, your opponent's reactions, everything that might influence the match. If you concentrate solely on the ball, a faulty stroke, or your footwork, your awareness of the true state of the match is restricted, and this can lead you to make the wrong shot selection on vital points.

If your Commentator Self is doing "his" job properly, you will not only have enough information to work out what you need to do, but also be able to anticipate what your opponent is going to do.

Anticipation: Another Key to Success

Anticipation is another vital ingredient of championship success. I am not merely concerned with the specific technical anticipation of whether your opponent's forehand is going mostly down the line or cross-court. I am more concerned that you establish a *feel* for what your opponent is likely to do on any given point. It is this feel that makes the top pros so fast.

The concept is very straightforward. By maintaining a constant awareness of the mental balance of the match, you can tell at any point whether your opponent is likely to hit out or play safe. Supposing you had pushed ahead psychologically and the mental balance is now 60–40 in your favor, the score 4–3, 30–15 yours. If you now pull your opponent wide to his backhand and come in, you know that he needs to do something to neutralize the mental advantage that you have built up. Therefore, the chances are he will go for the pass down the line (he has little cross-court angle), rather than lob. In the same way, if you're playing on a faster surface and you lead 4–1, 30–0 (mentally 80–20), and you have missed a first serve, the chances are strong that he will attack your second serve and maybe even come in (remember that no rule is always right, and this one is no exception; however, as the level of your competition gets higher, these tactics will become more consistent). In the first phase of junior tennis, when the players are physically small and the overhead is not a killing stroke, the lob is a very effective response to an incoming volleyer. As the kids get bigger and their overheads get stronger, the lob becomes less effective and the down-the-line pass begins to replace it.

As well as "feeling" what your opponent is likely to do, your Commentator Self should have been carefully watching what shots he prefers to make under specific conditions. Has he been going more frequently cross-court or down the line on his backhand passes? Have his volleys been mostly deep or short-angled? This information should all be fed into the Commentator Self to improve your anticipation and, even more important, to give you the ability to "fake him out," making him play a certain shot that you, being ready for it, can comfortably cut off. Say he has, under pressure, a preference for hitting his backhand passes cross-court, which you know from the points that you have already played. To shake his confidence as you come in again, fake him out by covering down the line slightly more than cross-court. This will tempt him into going for his favorite cross-court shot, which you can start moving for just as he commits himself. Often players who are thought to be fast simply anticipate well and so can start moving and preparing for the next shot that much earlier.

Reminders

- A champion is one who can win under any circumstances, whether the sun is in his eyes, whether there's a howling wind, or whether he is facing an opponent who is physically and technically stronger.
- If you concentrate solely on the ball, a faulty stroke, or your footwork, your awareness of the true state of the match is restricted, and this can lead you to make the wrong shot selection on vital points.
- By maintaining a constant awareness of the mental balance of the match, you can tell at any point whether your opponent is likely to hit out or play safe.

John McEnroe's Commentary

In the juniors you have to strike a balance between the mental and technical aspects of the game. I don't think you should go into a match just trying to hit great shots, playing the best style of tennis you can, and not caring about the result. You have to go in trying to win, being prepared to do whatever it takes to win. At the same time, you can't just forget about your strokes. Most kids want to go on to the pros, and getting there obviously involves having effective shots and using them in matches. A lot of kids with good competitive attitudes set themselves the goal of always getting the ball back, counting on their opponents' impatience or lack of experience to lead them to make a mistake eventually. They never try to do anything else, and even though it may win them a lot of points in their early tournaments, eventually they get blown away. They stand still because they never attempt to grow as players. In the pros the bottom line is winning; the pressure is always great, and there is not much time for worrying about developing a more varied game or trying out new shots. But in the juniors, where the pressures are less, you have to concentrate on constantly developing as a player and acquiring a more rounded game. If you are winning without developing, you will never be a champion.

When I was in the juniors I worked on my game so that it wouldn't have any weaknesses. I didn't worry so much about building enormous strengths, just getting rid of the weaknesses so that people didn't know for sure how to play against me. It is in the juniors that you learn how to win matches. It is fine to go out and play your own game if you think that you are better than your opponent, but if he starts beating you or you think he is stronger to start out with, you've got to try something different. Again, you'll have to strike a balance. I always try to play a game that is based on as many of my strengths as possible and at the same time attacks the maximum number of my opponent's weaknesses.

McEnroe's serve when he was a rookie in pro tennis, just before he changed to his trademark, the closed stance

Richard Pilling

When I beat Lendl in the WCT finals at Dallas, and earlier in Philadelphia, I played the type of game I feel most comfortable with. I had lost to him a string of times before because I had been trying to adapt my game too much to play his weaknesses (or, rather, to expose his weaknesses). In 1983 in both Dallas and Philadelphia, however, I decided to go more with my own strengths rather than playing to his weaknesses. And it worked. I started to come in and put pressure on his passing shots. Logically, you should beat a powerful player like Lendl by mixing it

McEnroe's superb volleys are the by-product of his determination coupled with sharp reactions.

Michael Cole

up, not allowing him to get grooved. But I had tried that in the past, and it hadn't worked. Therefore, you have to try something else. It makes no sense to keep doing the same thing if it's not winning for you.

4 PERCENTAGE THINKING

The Two Selves Technique will help you tap into the shifts in mental balance of the match, allowing you both to anticipate what your opponent is likely to do and to take the correct tactical steps to counter those moves. Once you have started feeling your opponent grooving mentally, or when you are pushing ahead, what do you do? How does it affect the way you play a specific shot?

Tennis is a game of percentages; both defensive and aggressive players use carefully selected high-percentage moves in order to win. Too many players think that high-percentage tennis means simply pushing the ball. At the same time, it is not unusual to find players who disregard the common sense of playing the percentages and indulge instead in flashy and risky tennis, which, by and large, results in an inconsistent record. I can remember talking to Ion Tiriac about the potential of the Frenchman Henri Leconte, who has all the technical talent anyone could ever want. When he is on, he can, and does, beat just about every good player in the world. But he blows hot and cold. He is either hitting screaming winners or losing left and right. He is not a true percentage player, at least not yet. True champions, like

McEnroe, Connors, Mats Wilander, and Borg, play percentage tennis and don't have such huge ups and downs.

What is a high-percentage shot? Simply a shot with a larger margin for error than most winners and therefore one with a greater likelihood of going in.

On the vast majority of points, if you can maintain a steady pressure on your opponent by hitting high-percentage shots, you will eventually force him to take the initiative with a low-percentage shot. Of course, there are occasions when a risky shot can be the correct one to play: when you're winning by a comfortable margin, say, and can afford it; or, equally, when you're losing and badly need to neutralize your opponent's mental advantage. However, in an even or a fairly close match, higher-percentage shots are a better bet.

Let's take a closer look at how percentage thinking applies to the major areas of your game.

Figure 4. Hitting your shots consistently to targets 1–5 will keep the opponent off balance and on the defensive (notice in each target the 1½-foot margin for error from the outer lines of the court).

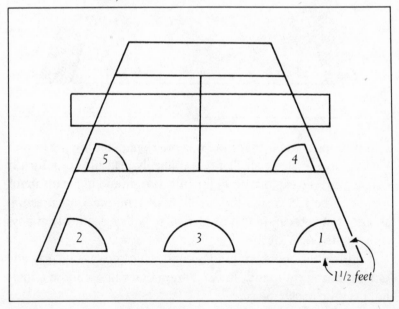

Pressing Shots

Too many juniors playing under pressure against an opponent at the net choose low-percentage passing shots, usually a panic-induced reflex to a situation in which they have to make a quick decision and get off the best shot possible as quickly as possible. From now on, start using the higher-percentage pressing shot instead.

Figure 5. Hit your pressing shots to targets 1F and 1B (forehand and backhand) rather than aiming for the shaded areas (lower-percentage passing shots).

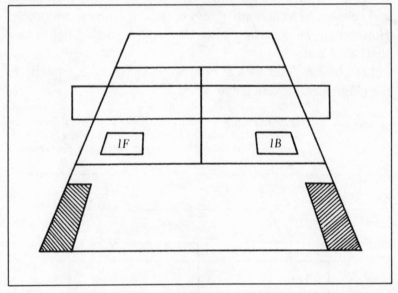

A pressing shot puts pressure on your opponent, forcing him to volley a low-angled ball that will probably lead him to return it defensively. To exploit this to the full, you should move up about two or three feet inside the baseline after hitting your pressing shot so that you can return his defensive volley as quickly as possible to the open court.

Should your opponent put you under pressure again, play another pressing shot, and, under extreme pressure, choose a high lob over the backhand side.

One of the most effective and consistent serves in the game's history

Michael Cole

Serve

If you get a high percentage of first serves in during a match, you put your opponent's returns under a lot of pressure. On the first serve, the mental balance is tipped in the server's direction, the receiver feeling slightly on the defensive, whereas on the second serve, the tables are turned, the pressure shifting to the server. So even if it means taking some of the pace off or putting a little more spin on your first serve, do it if it means you get more in. Generally, the higher your first-serve percentage, the lower the percentage of your opponent's returns.

Return of Serve

Consistently getting your opponent's serve back into court effectively neutralizes the psychological advantage he has when serving. It also has the effect of increasing the pressure on him to push

Figure 6. Use targets 1 and 2 to apply pressure on your opponent and when you approach behind a second serve. Use targets 4, 5, and 6 to apply pressure on his first volley. Use target 3 as the safest return against servers who stay back.

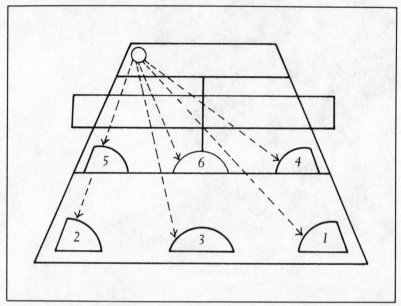

a little harder with his serve in order to counter your returns, and this often leads to a further reduction in his first-serve percentage.

There are certain things you can do to increase the percentage of your returns:

- Watch the ball from the moment your opponent starts bouncing it before serving.
- Have a target for every return.
- Keep moving your feet so that you can get a quick start.
- Shorten your preparation.
- Be aggressive and lean into the serve; even on an angled serve, step *in*.

Connors's aggressive returns can be devastating, even to the great servers.

Cheryl A. Traendly

The Stinger

A stinger is a shot that puts sufficient pressure on your opponent, forcing him to return it defensively and opening the court for your following shot(s) to win the point. Similar to the pressing shot but designed to apply pressure rather than defuse it, the major stinger in the modern game is the serve. For those who lack the power to make their serve a stinger, a deep and wide ground-stroke hit after a few exchanges can do the job, too. After hitting the stinger, you must move toward the target and, if it is a ground-stroke, about two to three feet inside the baseline, as for the press-ing shot. This allows you to take full advantage of a defensive return by striking it on the rise (or even by volleying it) and ex-ploiting your opponent's lack of balance and position to the full without your having to use a low-percentage shot.

In junior tennis, even at the highest level, you often see a kid hit an excellent stinger, only to miss the next shot. You have to remember that, before the point starts, there is about a 50–50 chance for either player to win it. As one player stings, his chances of winning increase (the amount depending upon the quality of his stinger), while those of his opponent decrease. As-suming you have a 75-percent chance of winning the point after your stinger, you don't need to hit a low-percentage shot to win it.

Figure 7. To cover your opponent's next shot most effectively, move to the middle of the widest shots (1 and 2) available to him. Move further forward on that line as you anticipate defensive shots.

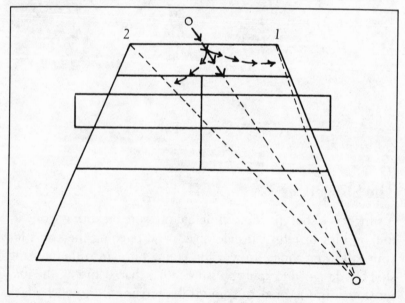

Figure 8. *Stinger to target 1 from position X. Player covers the return by positioning on X-1, and as quickly as possible delivers next shot to target 5 to put his opponent further out of balance (shaded area A is the most probable for his return). After execution of the shot, the player once again covers his opponent's next return (shaded area B) by positioning himself on X-2. Usually after the following shot to the stinger many possibilities are available (i.e., hit behind him, back to the diagonal targets 1 or 3, and so forth).*

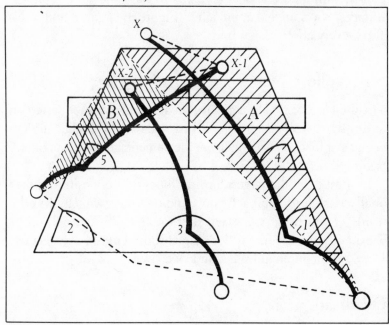

Simply continue the pressure with a higher-percentage shot, until you get a putaway. If your opponent neutralizes your stinger by lobbing or hitting a good low-percentage shot, then you must start carving the point again.

Approach Shots

An approach shot is just that, a shot that allows you to approach the net. It is not intended to be a winner. When approaching the net, shorten your preparation to build control, and generally go for flat or slice, rather than topspin, approaches. Slice and flat shots are quick and keep the ball low, which means your opponent has to hit up to you at the net. Topspins are slower and make the ball kick up, allowing him to hit it down at you. Also, on a slice shot your body momentum is naturally forward, whereas on heavy topspin shots the body momentum often pulls up and away from the shot. Generally speaking, on fast courts you want to approach with a deep shot (Figure 4: targets 1 and 2), but on slow surfaces, short angled approaches (Figure 4: targets 4 and 5) can also be very effective.

First Volleys

The pressure exerted by a good approach shot or a good serve continues when you make a good first volley. The higher the percentage of first volleys, the lower the percentage of the opponent's passing shots.

In most cases the targets for first volleys are opposite and diagonally related to approach shots and/or stinger targets. In other words, if you hit an approach shot to target 2 (Figure 4) on the backhand side, the first volley's target should most likely be target 1 or 4 on the forehand side. And vice versa.

Overheads

Your opponent's lob is usually a reaction to heavy pressure. A high-percentage overhead will maintain the pressure on him, increasing the chances of his hitting a defensive shot or a lower percentage shot. The deeper your opponent lobs, the deeper your overhead should be (Figure 4: target 1, 2, or 3).The shorter the lob, the more angled your overhead (Figure 4: target 4 or 5).

To get into the feel of high-percentage thinking, try practicing a drill I call the Penultimate Play Technique. The idea is very simple. Imagine that every shot you hit is a stinger and the set-up for a winner on the next shot. If you keep this in mind during the rally, you will get out of the habit that many otherwise gifted players fall into—namely, trying a ridiculously low-percentage shot at the worst possible moment. Because you are not actually trying to hit winners but are constantly working for an opening, you will build up a feeling for planning a point tactically rather than solely by instinct, and get used to using the percentages sensibly.

The Penultimate Play Technique is ideal either when you are in a neutral situation or when the match is beginning to go either way. But when your back is really up against the wall, you should consider a slightly different program called the Two-Ball Survival Kit. Again, the idea is simple. Let's say you are serving at 2-4, 15-40 and missed the first: simply say to yourself that you are not going to try anything other than high-percentage shots until you have played at least two shots after your second serve. This program also applies when you're returning a serve under similar scoring conditions. Until you have got those first two shots back, nothing must enter your mind except keeping the ball safely in play any way you can. Of course, if the opportunity arises you must take advantage and become more aggressive. The program is designed to get you into the big points, short-circuiting the tension and nerves by simplifying what is going on in your mind, giving your Player Self the simplest and highest percentage of goals—just keeping the ball in play. So often when players choke on a big point they become defensive and push the ball either for a mistake or for an easy set-up, or they try to get the point over and done with as fast as possible, pressing too hard too soon, and end up missing. If you use the Two-Ball Survival Kit on those points, on the other hand, your opponent may crack under the pressure and make a mistake first. You can bet that if you are nervous about a big point, so is he.

Finally, a word about errors. No matter how percentage-oriented your game becomes, you will always make a certain number of mistakes. Many players think that every time you make a mistake you should try to forget about it as quickly as possible. I recommend that you learn from them first. Just think of the TV commentators. What on earth would they have to talk about if they ignored all the players' mistakes? As it is, they feed off them, putting them into different categories and using the statistics to make judgments about how the players are reacting to the pressures of the match. It must be the same with your TV-Commentator Self. He must remember your mistakes, analyze them, and react to them. How he does it is important both to your tactics and to your mental attitude during the match.

There are three types of mistakes:

- The forced error: when your opponent puts you under so much pressure that you cannot handle his shot
- The forcing error: when you are playing a stinger or a pressing shot, not trying for a winner, but aiming to apply high-percentage pressure, and still miss it
- The unforced error: when, under no particular pressure from your opponent's shots, you make a mistake, often because of tension or lack of concentration

At the beginning of the match you already know that you will make a certain number of forced errors, depending upon how good your opponent is. In addition, you will also have a certain number of forcing errors, depending upon the ability of your opponent and your "feel" on the day of the match. Therefore unforced errors must be kept to a bare minimum: once added to the forced and forcing errors that you know you will make, they can make the difference between winning and losing.

Keep analyzing your mistakes, but instead of letting them depress you, try to figure out *why* they are occurring and take steps to cut them down. For instance, if you are missing too many first serves, reduce the power and put a bit more spin on the ball; if you are missing volleys, be more selective about your approach shots and aim to play two volleys instead of one to win the point.

Reminders

- Tennis is a game of percentages; both defensive and aggressive players use carefully selected high-percentage moves in order to win.

- A stinger is a shot that puts sufficient pressure on your opponent, forcing him to return it defensively and opening the court for your following shot(s) to win the point.
- You can bet that if you are nervous about a big point, so is your opponent.
- Unforced errors must be kept to a bare minimum: once added to the forced and forcing errors that you know you will make, they can make the difference between winning and losing.

John McEnroe's Commentary

As I've said, it is in the juniors that you learn how to win matches. The key to junior tennis is developing a game that doesn't have any glaring weaknesses, rather than trying to develop one with enormous strengths. That is basically what high-percentage thinking is about, especially at championship level: making it as difficult as you can for your opponent to beat you, not trying to blast winners the whole time. As you get older and bigger, and you start doing more with the ball and lasting longer out there, the game gets less defensive and more aggressive. But no matter what it looks like when you watch the pros play, it is never just blasting the ball up and down the court. The player is always thinking about how to neutralize the opponent's strengths while keeping his own mistakes to a bare minimum. The fact that you have played an opponent many times before does not stop the thinking. He may be playing better or worse than the last time, he may be trying something different, and you may be playing him on a different surface, his favorite perhaps, or one on which you haven't played him before.

The key to beating a player on his favorite surface, or on one that suits his natural game better than yours, is to get him out of his preferred game, make him do things he doesn't like to do. You can't just hope for victory; you have to do something different. The match I played against Guillermo Vilas in the finals of the 1981 Pepsi Grand Slam is a good example of this situation. Carlos was at that tournament with me, and after considering the court surface—which was *wet* clay—Vilas's game, and mine, we decided that I should come in with short, low-angled shots whenever I could and close in tight at the net to cover his topspin passes. During the rallies, I used heavier topspin than usual on my shots, until I got a decent opportunity to approach. The strategy worked, and I won that match.

When Borg retired two years ago, Connors could not beat him.

He had, as they say, Connors's number. But it hadn't always been like that. I'm sure that the turnaround happened when, having become mentally stronger, Borg realized that his game was as good as or better than Connors's.

On the pro circuit the game is very much a mental one. The juniors are a training ground for the circuit in every respect, right down to the traveling and scheduling, from the earliest tournament on. By the time you play the 18s you should have some idea of what being a pro can be. At the end of 1982 I was so tired that I didn't even feel like playing anymore. Junior players have to prepare mentally for all that grind; they have to be tough. Which is not to say that from the age of four on you have to grit your teeth and be deadly serious about tennis. If you lose in the second round of the National 14s, it isn't the end of the world, nor is it in the 16s or 18s. But as you get older it is important to be aware of the difficulties so they don't surprise you.

5
PACING A MATCH AND IDENTIFYING THE BIG POINTS

Imagine that an average player has just walked into the locker room having lost 6–3, 6–3 to the number-one seed, after having had his service broken three times. He is happy with the result, and one could assume it must have been a close match. In fact, it might not have been anything of the sort. Earlier I explained how true champions realize that they don't have to be perfect players to win. They don't have to win every match love and love, nor do they try to. They try to be at least good enough. And if you watch closely, you'll see that the times when they really turn it on are the key points in a match. They know which points they have to win and don't waste much energy winning the less important ones. So, in that 3-and-3 match, the number-one seed could have played at 70 percent in both sets, by pacing himself and winning the vital points in the three service-break games he needed. He might simply have paced himself better by winning the big points to secure the match. Who knows, he might have had his own reasons for not establishing a bigger lead earlier in the sets. Maybe he wanted to sharpen his "feel for the ball," save himself, or get a better taste for competition in the earlier rounds as he paced himself through the tournament. The point is that he advanced to the next round, and whether it was by three and three or love and love matters little as long as he got stronger to face his next challenger.

It would seem entirely reasonable to assume that in a tennis match every point is worth the same. However, the fact that we get tighter on certain points than on others suggests this is not entirely true. Some points, and games, are undoubtedly bigger than others.

It is important to remember that in tennis you can win a match even though you may win fewer points than your opponent. The difference is winning the big points.

How do you know when a big point is coming up? There are times during a match when the psychological edge is suddenly about to shift in favor of one or the other of the players. These shifts coincide with the big points; for example, 4–all, 30–all, which is one of the biggest points of a set.

People talk about the "vital seventh and ninth" games of a set as being the important ones. Why are they? Where is the mental shift? At 15–0 or 15–all, 2–1 or 2–0, the situation is basically still neutral. However, at 30–15 and 30–all, or 3–all, 4–2, or 4–all, one player either has or is about to move within a vital two-point or two-game margin. As a rule, any time one player is within two points of a game, or about to move within two games of a set, the mental balance begins to swing. So in the seventh game with the score 3–all, and the game score 30–15, you have a big game and a big point. If the server goes up 40–15, he has two chances to take a 4–3 lead, one break away from the set, thus putting the pressure on his opponent's next service game. Or, conversely, if the receiver wins the next point for 30–all, the pressure is on the server. If he wins again for a 30–40 lead, the mental advantage shifts firmly to him. If he then breaks to lead 4–3, he is serving for a 5–3 lead, and even if his opponent wins his next serve, he will then be serving next for the set. The same situation applies at 4–all.

What do you do on a big point? Though it is very difficult to generalize, a good way to understand it is to imagine a set of traffic lights. Generally speaking, every time you have two or more points than your opponent—that is, 40–0 or 30–0—that is a green light. If the score is even or within one point difference— 30–15, deuce—that's a yellow light. And if you're down two or more points—15–30 and, say, love 40—that's a red light. A green light means you can go for lower-percentage shots, a yellow light means you're better off playing the Penultimate Play Technique with stingers, and a red light means mostly high-percentage (Two-Ball Survival Kit and highly selective shots with a comfortable margin for error). And, in that vein, if the light is so red that the situation has turned black, you must shake your opponent's confidence and groove if you are to succeed. Under these circumstances, you should confidently play this red light as a yellow or a green, since you have little to lose and everything to gain.

If you follow these play patterns, your performance will communicate your wisdom to your opponent through emotional control, selectivity, versatility, and confidence—vital components of a winner.

Your Commentator Self is responsible for watching the lights, and he has to remember the difference between them. As with traffic lights, you can still cross the intersection on a yellow light, but you have to be more careful. So if you are serving at 4–3 and 30–love, you can try a lower-percentage passing shot if, for ex-

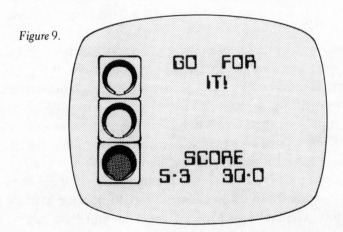

Figure 9.

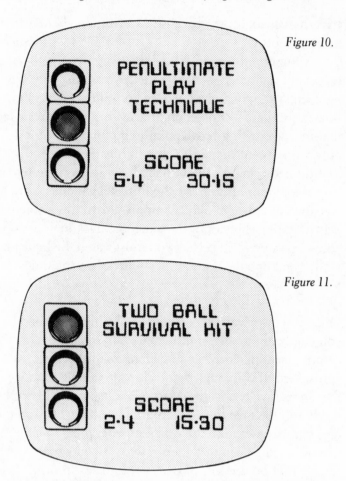

Figure 10.

Figure 11.

ample, your opponent chips and comes in. But if he wins that point and your lead is down to 30–15, the lights have changed and you should start using the Penultimate Play Technique.

The rule isn't unbreakable, of course. As you play more tournaments, you will realize that sometimes the light can be different in almost identical situations. If you have already won the first set and are ahead 4–3, 30–15 in the second, your light, though technically yellow, is almost a green, because the first-set victory has tipped the overall mental balance in your favor.

The first game of the second set and the first point of a big game have a special value, because by winning them you establish some authority.

It is important to understand that when you get a green light, especially against a good opponent, you must play it as a green light, not get tight and see it as red or yellow. Bjorn Borg recalled how in the 1977 Wimbledon final against Connors he led 4–0 in the final set, with a break point to go up 5–0. Although he had only a one-point margin in that fifth game, the 4–0 lead meant that he had a big green. But suddenly he became tentative and played for Connors to make the mistake, which is more typical of a yellow- or red-light play. Connors sensed this immediately and began nailing shots until he had come back to 4–all. The better your opponent is, the closer you must watch the lights, because a really good opponent always sees "light" on the other side of the tunnel.

Once you have learned to recognize the big points and big games, you can begin to use your mental and physical energy more efficiently, waiting for the crucial moments before really letting yourself go. If you watch the world's top middle-distance runners, the Steve Ovetts and the Mary Deckers, you will see how they rarely run the race from the front. They hang back on the shoulders of the leader until the vital moment, going into the last bend, when they dig deep into their reserves of energy and kick for the line. Don't be the sort of player who leads from the start at the cost of exhausting all of your reserves of energy, only to fade at the end. Learn to pace yourself. It takes experience, and junior tournaments are the best place to get it.

Once you are psyched up and about to start the match, what do you do? I remember a match McEnroe played in 1978 in the first round of the Mutual Benefit Life Open in South Orange, New Jersey, against Jay Lapidus, then a Princeton University player. Jay came out of the gates like a rocket, blasting winners left, right, and center, with very few unforced errors and only a handful of forcing errors. McEnroe, not at his best, decided the only thing he could do was to keep the ball in play, moving Lapidus from side to side, up and back. But he had little success. Lapidus raced through the first set and the first few games of the second, and then suddenly began to make mistakes. John kept hitting lots of balls, making him play every point. Jay broke down even more, eventually losing the second set and ultimately the match.

Really psyched, really feeling the ball, and excited by his early lead, Jay forgot to pace himself, succumbing to the temptation to go for it, like a dieter before a chocolate cake. Whether it was 15–0, 30–30, or McEnroe's ad, Lapidus was seeing green lights everywhere and blasting the ball. But John knew he couldn't keep it up. A lesser player might have given up and collapsed mentally, so that even when Jay finally did tire, he would not have been able to take advantage of it.

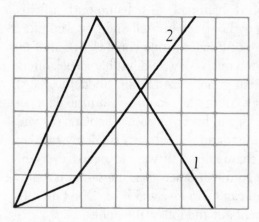

Figure 12. Hitting the wall: Player 1 rockets ahead and fades. Player 2 hangs in and gradually increases his performance as player 1 decreases his.

If your prematch routine and overall preparation are good, then you should be coming into matches really psyched. As the first games get going, feel your opponent out, use the Penultimate Play Technique to see what he's got, run on his shoulder, don't try to destroy him from point one. This strategy will give you time to work out any slight nervous tension you might be feeling early on, to start analyzing your opponent's mental, technical, and physical capabilities, and to build up your confidence and concentration. When you get your first green light, or even a yellow

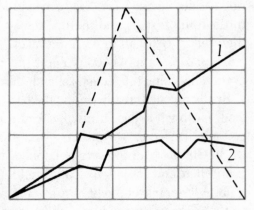

Figure 13. Revving up and down: Player 1 gradually builds his mental superiority and on the big points "revs up." He also realizes the need to rev down some to avoid hitting the wall.

one, and if you're feeling in the groove, then go for it, but as soon as the light has changed, rev down and pace yourself.

If you watch films of Muhammad Ali's championship fights, you will see how perfectly he paced himself and how versatile a fighter he was. Foreman or Frazier would come right out of the corner and blast away, and often Ali would just hang back on the ropes and let his opponent punch himself out. Suddenly, as Ali sensed the other's energy failing, he would give a little dance to re-establish the mental edge in his favor (just as Santana did with his drop shots against Mandarino), and then suddenly turn aggressive. Like all true champions, Ali was, in nearly every instance, always ready to go the distance. It is the same in tennis: never panic because you can't win love and love. Don't even try to. Just feel your opponent out and follow the lights.

Reminders

- There are times during a match when the psychological edge is suddenly about to shift in favor of one or the other of the players. These shifts coincide with the big points.
- Once you have learned to recognize the big points and big games, you can begin to use your mental and physical energy more efficiently.
- Learn to pace yourself.

John McEnroe's Commentary

My six-and-one-half-hour Davis Cup match against Wilander is
a perfect example of how the mental balance can keep switching
back and forth between two players and how you have to be able
to pace yourself in order to rev up and down at the right times.

It was an unusual match right from the start because you never
knew who was going to end up on top, and as it went on and on,
it became a struggle to see who could hold on longer. Having
come directly from Wimbledon, I went into the match really
tired. He was mentally and physically fresher than I was, and I
knew that he could probably last longer than I could. So I had
to try to take the earliest possible opportunity to finish him off
quickly. But I couldn't. I had a really good chance early in the
match but couldn't hold on to my lead, and once he had worn it
down and started pushing ahead, I could feel him building up
some real momentum. Suddenly, the match became an uphill
battle for me. On the other hand, it felt like more than just me
on the court playing him. Because it was Davis Cup, and because

*McEnroe's sense of patriotism has been shown during his
extremely successful performances in Davis Cup play. A
commendable commitment that he has honored since 1978.*

Cheryl A. Traendly

the match went on so long, I felt the whole crowd getting behind me. It was a pro-American crowd, which was an unusual experience in many of the Davis Cups I have played, and almost everyone stayed on to the bitter end. That really helped me hang on mentally.

At the start I was way up, as I said, but gradually Wilander came back and wiped out my mental advantage. By the time he had won the third set 17–15, he was way ahead mentally. I just couldn't get into the fourth set, and lost it easily. By the time we got to the fifth set, however, I felt we were back on more even terms. The whole match turned on one game in the fifth. My legs felt dead tired, but I sensed if I could only push just a bit harder, I would have him. Which is what happened. He played really well, and maybe the difference was that I had more Davis Cup experience than he, though that match was completely new to me, too. The point is that anything can happen in a tennis match. No matter how bad you feel or how bad the score looks, anything can still happen. You just have to hang on. Tough players have often come back to win matches that at one stage seemed hopelessly lost. Carlos mentioned my Jay Lapidus match, when I just hung in and didn't give up. But there was a bit more to that match, too. I had just lost in the finals of Wimbledon, so mentally I was down. Although I had won some major tournaments already, I had not yet won at Wimbledon and that loss was a big disappointment. Then came that first round against Lapidus. It was a clear case of a lower-ranked player playing above himself in order to beat a higher-ranked player that he is really hungry for. He was giving 110 percent. We had played in the juniors, so it also meant even more to him because suddenly I had become a big name. I started down and he started pumped up, but after a few games I began to get more into the match, and although I wasn't playing that well, I just hung on. I kept making him play, and eventually he got tired. Anything can happen; that is one of the most important things to remember.

Learning how to pace a match and learning how to pace a tournament are both vital, and for the ambitious kid what is even more important is learning how to pace his whole junior career. As I have said, there have been many cases of young players who have dominated the junior game, winning everything, only to fade away on the tour.

If you are going to win matches, you have to be a competitor, you really have to want to win. But you also have to treat this desire with care; otherwise you can burn it out. If you play too many tournaments too early and think about the game too much, you can drain your desire away. I have always been very competitive in everything I have ever done, but I didn't let tennis dominate me when I was a junior. I took months off from the game, played other sports like soccer and basketball, and always enjoyed my tennis. When you're a kid, you have to keep the game in perspective; you can't let it take over. On the tour it does take over because it's your living, but for a kid I feel it should just be a part of his life, rather than his whole life. An enjoyable part, not something that makes him miserable and his parents frustrated.

6 CHOKING

There are three feelings shared by all athletes, in every sport, at every level, and at every age: the exhilaration of winning, the disappointment of losing, and the agony of choking. Everything I have written so far shows you how to win more, but no matter how successful you become, there will always be times when you begin to choke or tighten up because of nervous tension. In the juniors it can happen often, so you have to know what to do and how to cope with it.

Choking is a perfectly normal reaction to pressure during which a metabolic change occurs, affecting your reflex and reaction time. Your heart starts beating faster, your breathing gets shallower, your muscles tighten, and your legs feel like lead.

On the tennis court this stiffness and sluggishness almost always occur on the big points, on yellow and red lights, and your ability to overcome this problem will be a deciding factor in your progress as a tournament competitor. Anybody can confidently play the point at 40–0 and 4–1, but many fewer can do so at 30–all and 3–all.

Although the tennis player may experience choking as a physical sensation, the roots of the reaction can be traced to the men-

McEnroe's expressive nature shows his feeling in all moments of a match.

Michael Cole

tal pressures that build up during a match. The key to overcoming it is to maintain a positive mental attitude. Never start fooling yourself by blaming your "rotten" strokes, whether it's your "uncontrollable backhand" or your "pathetic second serve"—"Of course I get nervous; my backhand's so bad, I always make mistakes just when it matters most"—or by simply giving up and pretending it doesn't matter anymore. You have to learn to tough it out. Champions are always prepared to let the match go the distance; they don't panic if they can't get a quick win.

I can't stress too much how important it is always to keep your attitude positive on the court. Be one of those irritating players who are never put out by bad luck or an off day. Moaning how badly you've been playing has a curious way of becoming a self-fulfilling prophecy. Conversely, if you shrug off the "bad-luck" shots and concentrate on the positive, that, too, often becomes self-fulfilling.

When McEnroe and Connors start feeling this mental tightening and their strokes begin to knot up, their reaction is suddenly to get very aggressive. This seemingly contradictory behavior serves two purposes. First, it loosens them up, stops the choking from becoming serious. Instead of starting to poke at the ball and pray for their opponents to make mistakes, they increase the frequency of their stingers and pressing shots, cloaking their nerves with a strong and aggressive mental attitude. Second, by becoming unexpectedly aggressive at a time when their opponents know the mental balance is very much against them or is delicately poised, they can often surprise these opponents into making mistakes or playing a defensive return, which they can then take advantage of. Watch McEnroe or Connors under pressure during a match. Watch how they pump themselves up, strutting across the court, wiggling their rackets from side to side—"It may be a red light, and you may think I'm tight, but watch out: you know that I just might go for it."

Because they are great champions, they can actually push the odds and the mental balance back in their favor by this sort of pumping up, in effect changing the lights from red back to yellow. However, most of you aren't a McEnroe or a Connors, at least not yet, so what should you do when you can feel yourself beginning to choke? Don't ignore the lights altogether and try to blast the ball, but do think more aggressively than defensively. Recognizing that it is a red light, get into the point using the Two-Ball Survival Kit, and then gradually switch to the Penultimate Play Technique as the exchange gets under way. As you become involved in the point, the tightness will gradually melt away; more important, you will have begun to dominate the mental dialogue with your opponent. He's nervous, and he knows you should be nervous. By showing courage when he's expecting you to push the ball, you really swing the mental balance away from him.

There are a series of well-tried methods that you can use to overcome the physical symptoms of choking:

- During your prematch routine, relax while you focus your attention, whether it is on having a rubdown, stretching, listening to music, or whatever. Sticking to the same routine before each match will also provide you with something familiar and therefore reassuring in an environment that can sometimes seem incredibly hostile.
- Realize that your opponent is experiencing the same pressure and stiffness, no matter how cool he looks. Even Borg admitted that he would get really nervous on big points, yet by acting cool, he allowed a myth to be built up around him, including the fact that his pulse rate was only 35 and dropped even lower as the pressure mounted. This just wasn't so. He was no more immune to tension than any other mortal. He was simply psyched more sharply to handle it.
- Take deep breaths while concentrating on relaxing your legs and shoulders; feel the muscles loosen as you concentrate.
- Keep your feet moving.
- Make an extra effort to keep your mind on the match, the ball, the weather conditions, your opponent's reactions, et cetera. And don't get bogged down in the "what if"s of choking. (What if I lose? What will my friends say? What will my parents say? What if I don't hold my serve?)
- Shift the pressure to your opponent by becoming more aggressive. Show him that you can tough him out!

All of these methods will help alleviate some of the symptoms of choking but will never eradicate them altogether. If you play competitive tennis, you will always be under some kind of pressure, and you must get used to that feeling and used to handling it. Having sat in the locker room with McEnroe before the finals of major tournaments, with tension seeping out of every crack in the walls, I know that anyone without a top pro's experience of

Tense moments for a tennis player

Tommy Hindley

coping with pressure—big pressure—wouldn't even have been able to walk down the tunnel to the stadium court.

Just as McEnroe has learned to tough it out by hard-won experience, so you must learn to tough it out by exposing yourself to competitive pressure at every opportunity you have on the tennis court. Even if you are relatively inexperienced in tournament play, you can build up your resilience to pressure by making your practice sessions more competitive, and by becoming more competitive in all the other games you play. When you are playing a game of basketball or chess, for that matter, go all out to win, put yourself on the line, and get tournament tough.

Reminders

- Although the tennis player may experience choking as a physical sensation, the roots of the reaction can be traced

to the mental pressures that build up during a match.
- Be one of those irritating players who are never put out by bad luck or an off day.
- Just as McEnroe has learned to tough it out by hard-won experience, so you must learn to tough it out by exposing yourself to competitive pressure at every opportunity you have on the tennis court.

John McEnroe's Commentary

When it comes to choking, the bottom line is that everyone does it. The question isn't whether or not you choke but how, when you do choke, you are going to handle it. A lot of players don't like to admit they choke. They feel uncomfortable about it, but it never really bothered me. If I choked, I didn't mind admitting it. Not worrying about choking certainly worked for me, though that doesn't necessarily mean that it will suit everyone else. Connors, for instance, doesn't like to talk about it; he keeps it private, and that has worked pretty well for him, too. But even if you don't admit it to anyone else, I think you should admit it to yourself; otherwise you won't know what really happened, won't be able to learn from it and cope better the next time it happens.

Learning from the times you choke doesn't mean learning how *not* to choke. As long as you play competitive tennis, it will happen to you at times. Juniors choke, and the top players in the world choke. Just look at Lendl in the final of the 1983 Open. Maybe it was a poor display; people have said that he gave up or that he wasn't fit. Yet I played him in the finals of Dallas a few months earlier, and at 5–5 in the fifth he was still running for every ball. The fact is that in the Open against Connors the pressure just got too much for him. He got so nervous that it exhausted him. That happens when you get tight; your legs go, they turn to lead. What had disappointed Lendl wasn't that he choked but that he couldn't handle it better, even though he had been in exactly the same position the previous year, again against Connors. He hadn't learned his lesson.

Choking is a big part of every sport, and part of being a champion is being able to cope with it better than everyone else. But there isn't any set way of doing it; everyone finds what's best for him.

Johan Kriek starts playing faster and faster when he gets tight. Other players do the opposite and start to stall. Still others begin to push the ball. Everyone is different. And that is just the point—everyone. It's the same whether I was playing Borg in the finals of Wimbledon or two juniors are playing in the first round of a local tournament. Choking at twelve feels very much the same as choking at twenty-four. Of course, the tension that causes it gets bigger. When you are playing on Centre Court in the finals, that's the ultimate tension. But the choking is basically the same.

7
THE SHOTS: BASIC MECHANICS

In 1968 professional tennis went through the biggest transition in its history, when the so-called "amateurs" and "professionals" of those days were allowed to compete in the same events. That marked the beginning of the "tennis boom." Since then there has been so much talk of technique that many players have drowned in it. Despite this increase in technical knowledge, a handful of pros have dominated the game year after year: Borg, Connors, McEnroe, Lendl, Vilas. Additions to this premier league come one at a time and at lengthy intervals, not in the rush that you might have expected with such widespread access to all this expert knowledge. In other words, the gap that separates the top six or seven from the rest of the field remains mental, not technical or physical.

It doesn't make sense to talk about correct or incorrect strokes, only effective and ineffective ones. Instead of worrying about form, understand that there are motions that the body can perform that deliver its full potential most efficiently. Simple body mechanics. An unorthodox style with basic mechanics could achieve full potential for some—Borg's forehand for instance, or McEnroe's serve. Both were regarded as freak shots to start with, and by many as seriously limited. But the critics were proved wrong and gradually changed their tune; now thousands of kids are serving with closed McEnroe stances and hitting with western and semiwestern "Borg" forehands. However, as I'll explain in detail later, this imitation can be dangerous, too, because, again, it comes from too much interest in form. The form-obsessed critics say the trend toward "individualistic" styles is bad. There are those to whom almost anything "new" is bad. Young people, however, generally like anything new and are equally fascinated by how things look (style), so they try to imitate the Borg forehand based on how it looks. Or they theorize: "If I stand the way McEnroe stands, then I'll serve as well as he does."

Wrong. What you need to do, whether you are analyzing or imitating a stroke, is first take a hard look to see if that motion feels comfortable to you. If it does, then go on to analyze the meat of the shot and forget the extra flourishes that make up the individual style.

Although there are almost as many styles as there are pros on the tour, all cleanly struck and effective shots have certain fundamentals in common. Beginning with groundstrokes, let us divide the swing into three sections to find out what they are:

1. Preparation
2. Production
3. Follow-through

The one thing that binds together all the top pros is the quality of their production (the eight inches after the initial contact, "the zip area"), the part of the swing in which the racket actually makes contact with the ball. However, many coaches continue to emphasize in their teaching the preparation and follow-through, which are mostly a matter of personal style. Their *sole* significance is to provide the proper distribution of momentum in the swing.

Many players and coaches believe that the bigger the "wind-up," or the preparation before contact with the ball, the more power the shot will have, and the greater the power after contact,

Figure 14. Preparation: Dotted lines show both large and small loop motions from the initial position to contact with the ball. The solid line is the optimum plane on which to contact the ball (just in front of the body).

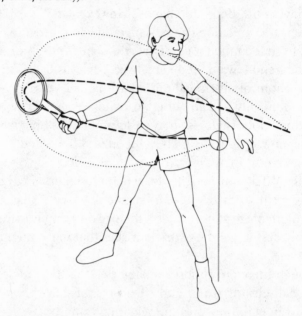

the less control you will have. Both beliefs are wrong. If all the power is concentrated in the preparation, the ball tends to fly off the strings too quickly, leading to a lack of control. If, on the other hand, you concentrate the power of your stroke on the precise instant when you contact the ball, the racket holds it longer on the strings, thus increasing your control. The reaction time is similar to what it is when you catch a ball in your hand. The moment the ball touches your palm, your fingers clamp tightly shut around it, stopping it from popping out again. A tennis stroke can be viewed in the same way, except that now the strings are the fingers. And to hold the ball when it touches the strings, the racket must be accelerating. This long contact is the feel for the ball that the top pros possess, and that everyone can learn. The key is simply to ensure that the momentum of the swing during production is greater than that prior to contact with the ball.

One very easy way of spotting how this momentum distribution

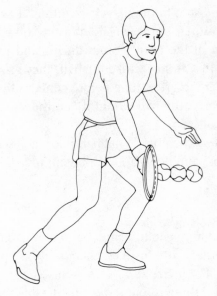

Figure 15. Production: From the moment of impact with the ball until the moment of release from the strings is the "when and where" of shot manufacturing.

Figure 16. Follow-through: The swing on the follow-through will move in accordance with the path of the swing during preparation and production. The body momentum during this phase of the swing should move toward the target of the shot.

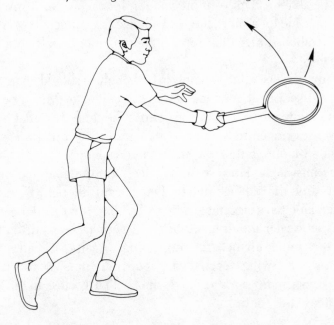

works in the pro game is to listen to the players grunting. These days almost everyone is grunting, but if you listen to it, you will notice that the loudest part of the grunt comes during and just after contact with the ball. Just as they stroke the ball, they grunt through the ball. If they were to grunt long before contact, thus focusing their energy too early, the ball would fly off the strings too quickly with little control.

So the key to sound strokes is timing. What part does each section of the swing play in this, and how can each be improved?

Preparation

The job of the preparation is simply to time and build up the momentum of the swing for contact with the ball as smoothly as possible. Provided it does this, the preparation can be any shape or any size. The most important thing is that it must be flexible; the court surface, the balls being used, weather conditions, and the ability of your opponent will all vary, and so the pace, direction, and bounce of the balls you receive will also vary. Therefore, you must be able to adapt your preparation for each shot. If you were running wide for a short, angled ball on a fast surface, it would be considerably shorter than for a high and straight ball on a slow surface.

Many players want to know whether they should loop their swings, like Lendl, or make them straight, like McEnroe's. It doesn't matter. Even McEnroe, who is thought of as a flat hitter, rarely uses an entirely straight swing. So the question is not "Should I loop?" but "How *much* should I loop?"

The answer is: However much feels comfortable and allows you to time the ball accurately. Once again, though, be careful about taking too exaggerated a loop. The bigger it is and the wider it is, the greater the distance between your racket and the ball, and the more chance for mistiming. Again, if you watch the pros, their swings, even the big loops of Lendl, Wilander, and Borg, under many circumstances are kept fairly close to the body to increase the control.

Borg's picture-perfect timing during preparation. Notice the control over his arm's swing.

Christopher Morrow

Bigger, wider swings tend to pull your body weight backward and sideways, when the only place you really want it to go is forward, through the ball and toward the target. Therefore, if in doubt, keep it shorter and smaller.

Production

As I have noted, the key to the production of any shot is concentrating the momentum of the swing just as and after you contact the ball. A good way of stretching out the contact, to hold the ball even longer on the strings and build up your "feel," is to think about hitting three balls instead of just one, lined up one after another, as if they were inside a can. Every time your shots begin to break down, come back to this exercise, focusing your swing during and after the initial contact and hitting through three balls.

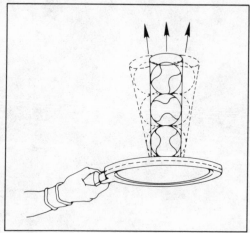

Figure 17. Three-ball contact: This visualization concept sharpens the "feel" for the ball.

Follow-through

If your preparation and production are well timed, then your follow-through will require no thought, it will simply happen—a natural winding down of the momentum generated during the previous portions of the swing. Following through is not just the

racket's work. Watching good strokes on slow-motion video replays, you will notice how perfectly timed is the combined transfer of both swing and body momentum through the shot. Be
careful not to start turning in to the ball too early, though; the
racket should lead your body weight toward the target. This synchronized physical and technical unit and the "feel" for the ball
are, in my view, the two most important fundamentals in developing effective shots.

These basic principles apply to every shot in the game, including the serve. They even apply to volleys. Many of you will have
been taught to block or punch volleys, but in fact you should
swing through on volleys, too; it is simply a smaller swing. The
power and control are still focused as and just after you contact
the ball. I am not saying to swing at the net the way you would
swing at the baseline. The swing on the volley usually takes place
farther in front of your body and generally downward, but it is still
a swing, not a prod. There are occasions when you can only
block—when the ball is slammed straight at you, for instance—
but you should swing through on any forcing or winning volley.

Reminders

- It doesn't make sense to talk about correct or incorrect
  strokes, only effective and ineffective ones.
- The key to the production of any shot is concentrating the
  momentum of the swing just as and after you contact the
  ball.
- Watching good strokes on slow-motion video replays, you
  will notice how perfectly timed is the combined transfer of
  both swing and body momentum through the shot.
- This synchronized physical and technical unit and the
  "feel" for the ball are, in my view, the two most important
  fundamentals in developing effective shots.

John McEnroe's Commentary

As far as strokes are concerned, what counts is not how hard you can hit the ball or how nice your strokes look, but whether you have a "feel" for the ball. Although some players seem to develop it more acutely than others, a "feel" can be learned, and all good players have it. I think about mental toughness in the same way. You can learn to be mentally tough, and that acquired toughness can take you a long way, even right into the top one hundred. But to be number one in the world you have to have something extra. Though hard work can take you a long way, very few can be at the very top. You will only find out how far you can go by going for it.

Coming back to your strokes, you need to build up your natural feel for the ball and the way it works for you. When you are a junior, you have to spend some time working on technique, you have to learn the basics that Carlos has described, and you don't need to worry about much more than that. When I play, I still think most about these basic concepts, and feeling that ball; they are so important.

Each individual has his own way of going about it. I probably couldn't hit the ball as hard as Connors did with his steel racket and still control it. The key, at any level, is to develop your own style, built on your natural abilities and feel. Everyone has a different feeling. Don't spoil yours by trying to make it into something it isn't.

8 FOOTWORK

Just as good strokes come from a good "feel" for the ball, good footwork is founded on a "feel" for the point. Because the ball is in constant motion, you must be in constant motion, too; yet many juniors, taught that some point three feet behind the baseline is their home base, rush slavishly back to that area after each shot and stop before setting off again. That is a waste of energy. Instead of stopping and starting, one should strive to achieve fluidity of motion.

"But if I keep rushing around the whole time, won't I wear myself out in a matter of games?" If you were to move inefficiently, you undoubtedly would, but the key to good footwork is to match your pace to the point. If you are dancing at a party and somebody puts a hard-rock tune on, it fits the beat to jump and throw yourself around, but if the next tune is slow, it would be ridiculous to keep moving at the same rate. You slow down. The same is true on the tennis court, except now the ball determines the beat. If it is fast, move quickly; if it is slow, move slowly. There is a lot of discussion on the tour about who is the fastest player in the game, and the votes are generally split among Borg, McEnroe, Kriek, and Vitas Gerulaitis. Next time you get a chance, watch how good their footwork is, how they stay so much in tune with the point mentally that their feet are always paced correctly, never entirely still, never tangled up. They move smoothly from one gear to the next. That's good footwork.

On return of serve you don't need to jump up and down frantically before every point. I see kids leaping up and down at 1–all, first set. Of course you have to be on your toes for every ball, but save the real psyching up for big points. Remember Steve Ovett and Mary Decker: save your energy for the final stretch.

The aim of your footwork should be to get to the ball quickly enough and in such a position that your body momentum can move through the ball toward the target. Poor footwork generally locks your body weight out of the shot, leaving just the arm to provide the power and control. "So what do I do when I've been forced wide or deep and can't move through the ball?"

McEnroe's racket control almost always enables him to come out of pressure situations.

Tommy Hindley

If your body weight is moving sideways or backward on contact with the ball (perfect definition of being under pressure), then you have to compensate with your arm, swinging more firmly and longer, leading your body back into position. Ideally, you shouldn't be in that position, although it does happen, no matter what level you're on. What is more important is finding out *why* you are in that position. It could be that your opponent has hit a very good shot that has forced you out of court, or it could be that because your footwork, along with your anticipation and feel for the point, was poor, you have in effect put *yourself* under pressure. If the latter is true, you need to pay greater attention to your physical training in order to build up your speed; the former requires that greater attention be given to the tactical level of the match.

As to the question about hitting with open or closed stance (lower body facing or sideways to the net), my answer remains: if it feels comfortable and it works, go ahead. There are enough examples of players succeeding on the tour with either stance to make any involved discussion of the point unnecessary. Just as with the preparation swing for your strokes, it is important to be versatile. Pulled wide and under pressure, you often have to hit off a stance that is either more open or more closed than if you had more time to get ready, so don't become so attached to a certain foot placement that you can't hit off anything else. If you prefer a closed stance, be careful that it isn't too closed, since this locks your body weight out of the shot. During open-stance strokes, the lack of power from your lower body must be compensated by coiling your upper body with your front shoulder.

Reminders

- Just as good strokes come from a good "feel" for the ball, good footwork is founded on a "feel" for the point.
- The aim of your footwork should be to get to the ball quickly enough and in such a position that your body momentum can move through the ball toward the target.

John McEnroe's Commentary

Footwork should never be underestimated. When you choke or when you're tired, the first thing that goes is your footwork. It's not something you learn once and never forget; you are always going to be working on it, improving and restoring it. During the U.S. Open in 1983, poor footwork was one of my main problems. It is a much more significant part of the game for some players than for others. For me it's vital. If my footwork and general mobility are bad, my whole game is pulled down. But if I'm able to move well and be on time for any shot, then my whole game is lifted. In the juniors I wasn't one of the fastest guys (though I wasn't one of the slowest, either), but as I got bigger and stronger, my speed improved. The reason I can get to balls that some players wouldn't isn't only that I'm quick but also that I anticipate well. Bjorn and Vitas are genuinely fast, and I probably couldn't race against them. But in tennis you don't need barn-burning speed to be able to get to tough shots if your anticipation is good. Again, it's mainly a mental thing that makes you get there. When you're tuned in to the game and have the desire to win the point, you'll start moving for shots before you can even see them.

9 THE COMPUTER PLAYER: NEW TRENDS

The international tennis circuit is now run by computers. Teenage kids are breaking codes of nuclear-power stations, banks, and hospitals with the personal computers in their bedrooms. A recent study identified the fastest-growing segment of the personal computing market as educational software and hardware for use in schools, and predicted that the present demand will increase fourteen times by 1987. In other words, the next generation of tennis pros will have grown up in a world where bubble gum and apple pie have been replaced by rams, bytes, and BASIC, where you learn from computers, play with computers, and communicate with computers. How is the silicon chip going to affect their performance on the tennis court, and can the computer-conscious junior convert his soft- and hardware into extra points and games against his opponent?

Until a few years ago the most important technological advances in the game had come in racket design and footwear. Martina Navratilova helped bring technology into the game itself, thus adding a new dimension to tennis. She built herself into an almost invincible player partially by using computer-based systems that regulated her diet and analyzed her opponents' games

73

(and her own) for strengths and weaknesses. What can you do with your computer that will help you?

A number of programs are already on the market with names like Tennis Metrics, Computennis, Tennis Stat, and Promatch, all of which are designed to analyze your opponents' game as well as your own. This software breaks your game down into percentages, and the more of your matches you feed in, the more detailed the analysis becomes.

Some of the results that have emerged from these computer studies of top players are fascinating. For instance, Jimmy Connors is regarded as perhaps the best returner of serve in the game. Yet, throughout his five matches in the Alan King Classic in Las Vegas early in 1983, he won only 33.2 percent of points off his opponents' first serves. That puts him somewhere in the middle of the pro pack. However, with a score of 69.2 percent of points won off their *second* serves, against only 47.9 percent for his opponents off his second serves, he emerged far in the lead.

A much better way to utilize this software, rather than just working out service patterns or determining whether a player wins most of his points at net or in the back court, would be to record and break down a player's performance on red, yellow, and green lights. If you were to get a clear idea of how many points a player won under specific types of pressure, you would begin to have a statistical record of how tournament tough he was. It would also work very well if you had a team of researchers feeding information into the computer about your or your opponents' matches, but for the junior that is simply not practical.

There is also more sophisticated software available. Using a high-speed camera, a biomechanical analyst, and a digital computer with a special program, it is now possible to show discrepancies between a tennis player's swing and a theoretically perfect model. Because the results can be viewed on the screen, this brings the analysis much more to life and opens up the possibility of getting a "feel" for the correction by watching an animated figure going through both swings. However, this is only dealing with the purely technical, doing something that a good coach and a video camera could do much more simply at far less expense.

Nonetheless, I believe that computers can help you become a better tennis player and that in time their involvement in tennis is inevitable. The reason is simple: they are becoming a part of our development. In schools, computers are now being used to teach children directly, with amazing success. The students learn faster, retain the knowledge longer, and, most important, *enjoy* learning more. Computers are affecting attitude. A recent report by the Office of Technology Assessment (the analytical arm of the U.S. Congress) listed a series of studies that showed that "Through the detailed and highly individual feedback provided by the computer, computer-aided instruction in schools helped students acquire habits of precision in their work . . . and in the cases of underprivileged kids, increased their motivation to learn, while cutting down on vandalism."

How does all this affect your tennis game? Playing and learning with computers is making kids tougher mentally, making them more organized, more analytical, more flexible. These are some of the same qualities that underlie tournament toughness. In addition, by helping kids learn better and faster, computers are cutting down the amount of time required for homework, which gives the junior player more time on court. One fourteen-year-old junior I work with organizes his schoolwork through his personal computer, maintaining good grades (which delights his parents) and giving him more time for tennis. The result has been a great leap in his ranking, more support from his family (both emotional and economic), and a happier kid. He has also become very good at video games, which has helped to improve his reaction time on court and build up his confidence.

With video-game consoles that can double as personal computers by having a keyboard slotted over the top (ideal for learning the ropes while you play the games), there is now equipment available for all ages and most income brackets. So try to get access to a computer; use it to help out with schoolwork, to practice your video-game skills whenever you get a chance, and get the triple kick of having fun, pleasing your parents, and toughening up your mental attitude.

Reminders

- The next generation of tennis pros will have grown up in a world where bubble gum and apple pie have been replaced by rams, bytes, and BASIC, where you learn from computers, play with computers, and communicate with computers.
- Playing and learning with computers is making kids tougher mentally, making them more organized, more analytical, more flexible.
- These are some of the same qualities that underlie tournament toughness.

10 *TENNIS-FIT*

Junior tennis players often get a little confused when it comes to getting fit for the game. Training is important, but some young players go overboard with it. Naturally, the fitter you are, the more effective you become on the tennis court, but before embarking on a frantic program you should understand how being "tennis-fit" is different from being fit for many other sports. Despite what you may have read about Chip Hooper's pumping iron to build up his serve and overhead, tennis does not require the same kind of overwhelming physical strength that's needed in boxing, wrestling, shot-putting, or football. Neither McEnroe, Connors, nor Borg looks like Charles Atlas, yet they are the tennis strongmen, while Victor Amaya, Chip Hooper, and others who are far bigger and stronger lag far behind in the world rankings.

I don't mean to discount entirely the use of weight training. I just want to put it into perspective. Generally speaking, the tennis body is lean and wiry, rather than bulky and muscle-bound. If you were simply to play tennis and do little or no off-court conditioning, you would naturally tend to develop your body the former way, because all your exercise would be isotonic; that is, the muscles would develop by repetitive action against low resistance (hitting and running after the ball time after time). Lifting weights, on the other hand, generally provides isometric exercise, in which the muscles move short distances against high resistance, building muscle bulk and decreasing flexibility.

Nonetheless, training with weights can be beneficial to the tennis player, *provided* that it is part of a carefully designed program that takes into account your weight and age. Like all training, it tests and steels your motivation while building your determination, and in Hooper's case it bestowed a devastating, explosive power that made his serve and overhead frequently unreturnable. In addition, it can build your muscles' endurance and thereby your ability to handle a long match. In the fifth set at 5–5, with the temperature in the 90s and no sign of a service break, physical strength can be all-important.

Many of the players who now work out with weights do so as an injury-prevention measure, and not only because they think it will improve their game. Where once they waited until they were injured before pumping a little therapeutic iron, now many of them work out to build up their strength where they have a weakness and therefore are susceptible to injury.

Nautilus training is ideal, combining many of the benefits of conventional weight training with those of isotonic exercise. On the machines your muscles are made to work through the full range of their motion, thereby avoiding the build-up of inflexible bulk. Nautilus training has been used successfully by many pros, including Gene Mayer, Pam Shriver, and Billie Jean King, and the fact that Jimmy Arias during his junior years as well as other top-ranked juniors have found it so beneficial suggests that it can be helpful for teen players.

The key, as always, is moderation. The availability of Nautilus and of expert instruction can make it a viable addition to any junior's training program. The fact is, however, with a ball that weighs one and a half ounces, a net that is only three feet high, and a court that is seventy-eight feet long, you don't need brute force to play out a point.

Tennis fitness can be divided into three main areas:

• Mental-motor responses
• Stamina
• Speed

Underlying them all is flexibility. I don't intend to lay out an eight-week training program, with scores of exercises and drills to be performed in increasing amounts until at the end you can split your T-shirt by taking a deep breath. That's up to you. What I will do is explain how each of the areas can improve your game and give you some suggestions about how to develop all three, which you can then build into your own training program.

The first thing to remember is that physical training doesn't always have to be a chore. I've already mentioned the fact that sports requiring "bulking up" as part of their training are not really compatible with tennis, but a lot of others (especially basketball, soccer, and skating) provide ideal and enjoyable ways of getting tennis-fit. Both McEnroe and Fleming relate how they used to play other sports besides tennis, and how important it is not to cut yourself off from all your non-tennis friends. Don't let your whole life revolve around tennis. Playing other sports is a perfect compromise. It gives you access to activities and friendships outside tennis, while at the same time it gives you the kick of knowing that you are not just playing basketball or soccer with your friends but are also building up the *quick eyes*, *quick hands*, and *quick feet* that make you a better tennis player. Remember, Bjorn Borg was brought up on table tennis and ice hockey, and McEnroe played both varsity soccer and basketball during his high-school years.

Mental-Motor Responses

This is a pseudo-scientific term that refers to the passing of commands from your brain to your muscles. Say you've chipped and come in to the net, and your opponent blasts a forehand right at you. Your brain screams out a command to your racket arm (and

Borg's demonstration of his athletic capabilities

World Tennis

your feet, legs, and neck, too) to get the racket head to the path of the ball before the ball hits you or rockets by. Naturally, the faster those responses, the more effective your volley. Playing video games is an excellent way of developing your hand-eye reaction time, and running tires the way preseason footballers do builds up the response of your feet.

Stamina

Stamina is your ability to endure strenuous physical activity over an extended period. McEnroe showed how much stamina he had by beating Mats Wilander in the Davis Cup match that lasted over six and a half hours. Knowing that your body isn't going to give up on you under the normal circumstances of a match, that you can stay out on the court all day if you have to, gives you a great mental boost in close matches and stops you from panicking when you realize that you are not going to get a quick two-set victory.

It is important to understand that even though you may be able to play three to five "practice" sets, playing under tournament conditions could be more physically demanding because of the added mental pressure. Your muscles become less flexible, your heart beats faster, and a rally that wouldn't seem anything special in practice can really take it out of you at 3–all, 30–all, final set.

That is why it is important to make your practices as competitive as possible. Whenever you get a chance, play points in the same spirit that you would play a match; don't just hit and play "friendlies."

Long-distance running is also effective: physically, by exercising your legs and your cardiovascular system, and mentally, by setting you a goal (say, three miles) that requires determination to achieve. Thus, running builds up physical as well as mental stamina.

Speed

In tennis it is not so much speed as quickness that counts—the ability to anticipate well, to react quickly, change direction, and recover for the next shot. Vitas Gerulaitis is a perfect example of this quickness. There are a hundred different ways of building up quickness—running tires, jumping rope, running the lines on the court—all of them very effective. I particularly like to see kids training on the court, because the more time you spend productively on it, the better you know it. But a mixture of all the "agility drills" you can find is the best solution, for it breaks up the monotony that a lot of kids build into their training programs (the same exercises in the same sequence, week after week).

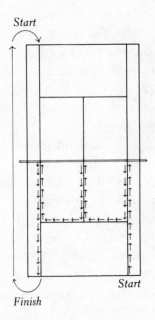

Figure 18. *Quickness: Run as quickly as you can following the arrows (touch the net with your racket). Be sure to run backward from the net, simulating a run for overheads.*

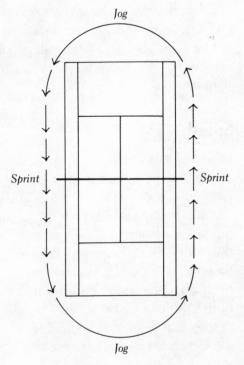

Figure 19. *Speed and endurance: Sprint along the sides of the court and jog along the back fences. Increase the amount of sprinting as your fitness improves.*

Cheryl A. Traendly

Gerulaitis: *always on his toes*

Stretching

Most youngsters just starting the first stage of junior tennis are naturally very flexible. They start slowly and gradually, allowing their bodies to warm up. As we get older and more ambitious, it is easy to lose that natural flexibility and natural warming up. The result can be a shower of injuries, which, if they occur in the early teens, can be very serious and impair subsequent development.

Before and *after* every match or practice session, you should stretch out. Peter Fleming has provided a good example to many

Fleming's stretching session

Bill Epridge

juniors I've coached for his discipline in this area. Before and after his workouts and matches he spends a considerable amount of time on his stretching routine.

The pros rely on their bodies to perform at their best week after week, and they know how to look after them. You should get into the same frame of mind. Get into the habit of stretching before and after every match and practice session, and don't find excuses to let it slide because you don't have time or just can't be bothered. Many kids feel self-conscious about stretching out on the court at tournaments. If you do, then stretch out in the locker room before the match. Never forgo it. At big pro events, even though you don't ever see the players stretching out, you can be sure that everyone in the draw has stretched in the locker room, and many have had a rubdown as well.

Reminders

- Neither McEnroe, Connors, nor Borg looks like Charles Atlas, yet they are the tennis strongmen, while Victor Amaya, Chip Hooper, and others who are far bigger and stronger lag far behind in world ranking.

• Many of the players who now work out with weights do so as an injury-prevention measure, not only because they think it will improve their game.

• The availability of Nautilus and of expert instruction can make it a viable addition to any junior's training program.

• The first thing to remember is that physical training doesn't always have to be a chore.

• A lot of other sports (especially basketball, soccer, and skating) provide ideal and enjoyable ways of getting tennis-fit.

• Even though you may be able to play three to five "practice" sets, playing under tournament conditions could be more physically demanding because of the added mental pressure.

• In tennis it is not so much speed as quickness that counts— the ability to anticipate well, to react quickly, change direction, and recover for the next shot.

• Before and *after* every match or practice session, you should stretch out.

John McEnroe's Commentary

I don't believe that lifting weights is very helpful in becoming a good tennis player. Being physically big and strong isn't one of the prerequisites for winning a match. I'm not enormous, and neither is Connors or Borg. The fact is that tennis players don't need to be as physically big as some other athletes. We're not like wrestlers; we don't physically fight each other. We need to be fast and to be able to change direction quickly. Excessive physical training doesn't help a tennis player nearly as much as it does some other athletes. Personally, I've found that having played other sports has helped much more than simply working out. I don't play them that much now, both because I don't want to take the risk of getting injured and because it's hard to find the time. But when I was younger, I used to play basketball and soccer. They helped my overall conditioning and also gave me a break from tennis. I made some new friends outside of the game and kept my life more balanced, but I was still able to keep up the competition. It's so good for kids to do more than simply play tennis. You need to get away from it every now and then.

11 ESPECIALLY FOR GIRLS

by Mary Carillo

The first and most important point this book makes is that winning tennis matches is at least as much about competitive attitude as it is about physical or technical ability. That attitude is no different for a female player.

There are simply not enough important differences between a man's game and a woman's game to make a fully detailed, separate attack necessary. The collection of voices in *Tournament Tough* is speaking universal truths about the game, which apply equally to all tennis players, whatever their sex. Perhaps ten or fifteen years ago it would have been important to have a section specifically for girls, but the game is no longer so lopsided.

While the acceptance of professionalism and participation by women in a whole range of sports has increased, tennis has been by far the most successful. In 1970, Gladys Heldman—one of the chief proponents of the women's game—persuaded Phillip Morris to sponsor (for $2,500) a women's-only tennis event . . . the first Virginia Slims. Billie Jean King, together with a group of seven other professionals, pioneered in the establishment of a women's tour, which in 1982 was worth $11 million.

At present the women's game, even more than the men's, is

Mary Carillo during one of her television broadcasting sessions

Cheryl A. Traendly

dominated by the issue of child professionalism. Ever since the then sixteen-year-old Chris Evert burst on the scene in 1973 by reaching the semi's of the U.S. Open, professional tennis has seen younger and younger players: Austin, Shriver, Mandlikova, Jaeger, Rinaldi, Bassett, and many others who turn pro while still in their middle teens.

This issue raises many intriguing questions, ranging from the ability of scarcely adolescent bodies to withstand the sheer physical toll of life on the tour (in the light of Tracy Austin's enforced temporary retirement from the game, due to injuries, at the age of twenty) to doubts about the quality of life enjoyed by players who miss out on their adolescence and higher education. However, to the vast majority of junior girl players this is not a live issue, just an academic one. The handful of teen-age players who manage to succeed on the pro tour are exceptional talents.

If a girl's game is still maturing, still improving, and especially if it still has holes in it, that player is a perfect candidate for college tennis. It is difficult to improve on the tour. There is just too

Billie Jean King, the pioneer of modern women's tennis, has contributed immensely to bringing the women's game to the forefront.

Cheryl A. Traendly

much pressure, too little practice time, too much nose-to-nose competing, comparing.

All too often I have seen bright, young talents with marvelous potential arrive on the pro scene and get so caught up in the pressures that they stunt their growth and fall back on what they know best—the game they brought with them. All their wonderful potential dries on the vine; they feel too rushed, too pressured, to nurture their game along slowly.

I would not recommend pro tennis to any girl—or, for that

Chris Evert Lloyd was able to benefit from Billie Jean's trailblazing, then took the women's game even further, making it universally accepted as a prime field for women's aspirations.

Cheryl A. Traendly

Alycia Moulton, a fine college
player who has successfully
alternated school with her
tour schedule

Cheryl A. Traendly

Carling Bassett and Andrea
Temesvari, two shots in the
arm that women's tennis has
sorely needed since Martina
Navratilova's strict domination. Both are confident,
gutsy, and bright.

Michael Cole

matter, to any boy—who thinks of it as a kind of on-the-job training. Before you join the professionals, make sure that you are one in every possible way—that you think like a professional athlete, live like one, and play like one. If you have not yet reached that point, find a good tennis college with a strong coach and give yourself a little more time. With more than seven hundred colleges and universities offering thousands of athletic scholarships, the opportunities for the ambitious girl player today are greater than ever.

In summary, my views on the relationship between the boys' and girls' games are very straightforward. Should a girl train with boys? Sure. She should train with the best talent around, boy or girl. Should she engage in a weight training program? Sensible weight training, as it was explained in the previous chapter, can be beneficial to all athletes.

Should girls play an all-around game? Absolutely. The 1970s were years of baseline dominance, of Borg and Evert. In the

Navratilova restructured the women's game.

Michael Cole

1980s, the best—McEnroe, Navratilova—play it all over the court. They are this generation's role models in tennis, and they are pointing to the future of the game—bigger, faster, harder, better.

Last year, when I was in the midst of writing the book I did with Martina Navratilova, she looked up from our notes and said, "Why are we limiting this to women? Anyone who reads this will learn from it." So we shifted gears a little and opened it up. *Tournament Tough* speaks to both boys and girls with equal effectiveness. There are no special rules. The bottom line is that they *all* want to be good.

12 NUTRITION FOR THE JUNIOR PLAYER

by Dr. Irving Glick

Nowadays when people talk about diet, most of them are thinking about losing weight; but when an athlete talks about diet, he's referring to nutrition. Good nutrition, along with a balanced program of physical training, helps a junior player to achieve his full potential. Next time you're about to sink your teeth into a pre-game hamburger and bag of French fries, pause to consider the importance of good nutrition. Although no diet can actually make you win a match, a bad diet can contribute considerably to a poor performance.

The aim of good nutrition is to provide the best-quality fuel for your muscles to burn. The aim of fitness is to enable the body to feed that fuel faster and more efficiently and to improve the muscles' ability to store and to burn the fuel. A weakness in either—nutrition or fitness—affects the other. If you give your muscles poor fuel, they will not function at their best. In the same way, if your body is out of condition, no matter how good a diet you have, the muscles will not be able to take advantage of it. Too many young athletes will willingly spend hours training their bodies only to sit down to a junk-food feast to take the edge off their hunger. If you are serious about your tennis and are looking to gain every possible edge over your opponents, take a closer look at what you are eating and drinking.

Though nutrition is important, it is not complicated, despite the dizzying variety of "energy" foods and vitamin and mineral supplements now available. The body can be kept healthy with good basic foods: milk, eggs, meat, fish, poultry, fresh fruit and vegetables. Nor do the principles of good nutrition vary from athlete to office clerk. The major difference is that people who are physically active require more calories and fluids.

The body is always burning up fuel, even during sleep. What are the types of food, and how do they help or hinder the athlete?

Food can be broken down into six parts, each with different functions: *water, carbohydrates, fat, protein, minerals* and *vitamins*. All we shall consider here is how important each one is for a tennis player, and which prove to be the best sources of energy.

Water

Water is all around us and is so easily available that we tend to take it for granted. Water is used by every cell in our bodies and is necessary for the proper functioning of our bodies' mechanism—and even for survival. Maintaining adequate water and mineral content of the body is essential for peak athletic performance. Intensive physical activity produces sweating, causing water loss. Excessive water loss can reduce one's endurance and the efficiency of one's performance. Drinking liquids such as water and fruit juices helps guard against dehydration.

Even an inactive person needs six glasses of water or other fluid a day. With increased activity, more water is required. Always make a point of drinking at least one glass of liquid with each meal and whenever you are thirsty. If you fail to keep your body supplied with enough fluid, you may rapidly become dizzy and tired, and in very hot or humid climates will run the risk of sunstroke.

A half hour before practice or before a tennis match, I recommend one to two glasses of water. At every changeover between

Cheryl A. Traendly

There are many ways of cooling off during matches on hot and muggy days.

Mary Valentine

games, it is wise to have a cup of water. It is practically impossible to drink too much water. Fruit juices equally diluted with water are quite helpful in a prolonged match—after the first hour of play—in providing hydration and an energy source. Cool water is absorbed more quickly from the stomach. During hot weather, the cool water also helps cool the body.

Carbohydrates

Carbohydrates are the main fuel for exercise. There are two forms of carbohydrates: simple carbohydrates or sugars, and complex carbohydrates or starches. The simple carbohydrates are found in candies, jellies, syrups, honey, et cetera. The complex carbohydrates or starches are found in vegetables, potatoes, cereals, flour, pastas, et cetera. The simple carbohydrates pass from the intestine straight into the blood stream. However, the complex carbohydrates or starches are broken down slowly in the body. These complex carbohydrates can be stored in the liver and when necessary can provide a source of fuel. This means that the energy boost you can get from these foods is long-lasting, in contrast to the sudden peak and drop-off from sugars. The latter, while providing an initial energy boost, raise the level of insulin, ultimately causing a lower blood-sugar rate, which is undesirable for prolonged and peak performance.

Fats

Fats, which provide a secondary source of energy after carbohydrates and proteins, can be stored in the body (in muscles, around organs, and under the skin). The main source of fuel when the body is resting, and also in the later stages of endurance sports, fats contain about twice as many calories as carbohydrates and proteins. When a person exercises, he or she requires carbohydrates for energy. When the carbohydrate stores are depleted, then fats are required to fuel the body. There are two types of fats: the saturated and the unsaturated. The virtues of unsaturated fats such as margarine and peanut and vegetable oils have been well popularized in the media. The evidence that saturated fats play a role in high cholesterol levels has been well established, and the intake of saturated fats should be limited. Saturated fats are found in red meats, butter, and cheese.

Protein

Protein forms the basic structural material of the body's cells and can be found in such foods as meat, fish, poultry, eggs, peanut butter, milk, dried beans, and wheat. Its function is to build and repair damaged tissue and muscle. Protein cannot be stored in the body. If it is not used by the body immediately after it is consumed, it is broken down by the liver and is excreted by the kidneys in the urine. If more protein is eaten than the body can use, the kidneys and liver are required to work harder, diverting blood to the kidneys. The elimination of broken-down protein through the kidneys requires increased water, to get rid of the end products in the urine; this may hinder athletic performance, because the job of breaking down protein imposes a greater load on the kidneys, taking blood from the working muscles and stomach. Further, the athlete who eats a lot of protein has less room for carbohydrates, which provide the fuel for the athlete's machine. Protein requirements in the diet do not increase with exercise. Before protein is absorbed into the bloodstream, it is broken down into basic building blocks called amino acids. When there is carbohydrate depletion, protein can contribute 10 percent of energy production. In active, well-nourished athletes, protein contributes little to energy production.

Minerals and Vitamins

In theory, there is generally no need for vitamin and mineral supplements if one consumes a balanced diet; however, the stress of daily life, and the loss of minerals and vitamins in modern food processing and preparation, deprive many foods of their vitamin and mineral content. Eating at irregular hours makes it more difficult to obtain the balance of nutritious foods. Consequently, I feel it is important to take a reputable, well-balanced multi-vitamin-and-mineral preparation daily. In caring for world-class athletes during strenuous tournaments and in hot weather, I increase the mineral intake to compensate for loss through dehydration. As previously mentioned, increased fluid intake is necessary as well. Minerals, including trace elements, help ensure proper heart function, prevent fatigue, and guard against muscle cramps.

After considering these six components of food, the questions arise: What should we eat, and what constitutes a nutritious diet?

A good diet would be broken up as follows: 60–70 percent complex carbohydrates, 20 percent protein, and the rest fat, along with some liquids. Junior players should try to cut down on their consumption of sugar, as is found in sodas and candy. Instead, they should satisfy their sweet tooth with fruit, a complex carbohydrate, which is ideal. They should also replace junk-food snacks with bananas or grapes. If the craving for fast food is overwhelming, try to get used to low-fat foods such as chicken and fish sandwiches and salads. Fried foods and fatty dressings such as mayonnaise should be avoided. Remember, make a point of drinking often, and always before you begin to play and at changeovers. This leads us to consider the requirements of the pregame meal.

Your pregame meal should satisfy all the principles of good nutrition—should, namely:

- Be high in complex carbohydrates but low in sugar
- Be low in protein and fat
- Contain several glasses of liquid
- Be easily digestible

An example of a pregame meal would be: two glasses of fruit juice, cereal with skimmed milk, a piece of toast with a little margarine, and potatoes. Allow about three hours between eating and playing. It is always best to exercise with an empty stomach; otherwise you risk cramps.

In summary, for an improved and more nutritious diet, I recommend the following:

- Eat more fruits, vegetables, and whole grains, which provide fiber.
- Eat less red meat but more poultry and fish.
- Eat less high-fat food. Partially replace fatty foods with foods containing unsaturated fats, such as chicken and fish for pork, margarine for butter.
- Drink low-fat milk instead of whole milk.
- Avoid highly sugared foods and drinks.
- Cut down on salt and on food with high salt content.
- Be sure to eat a proper breakfast. There is considerable scientific evidence demonstrating increased efficiency after eating breakfast. Studies also demonstrate that people who eat a wholesome breakfast have a longer life span.

13 PLAYING TOURNAMENTS

I'm always surprised at how many juniors, however mature they are in other respects, haven't a clue when it comes to organizing themselves sensibly for tournament play. This may be partly because when you watch a major pro tournament you haven't seen the players preparing for it. You only see them walking out onto the court, warming up for a few minutes, then starting play. You do not see them planning their tournament schedules or making their travel arrangements. Their names just keep appearing in the sports columns of the newspapers as if by magic. In fact, for someone like John McEnroe, organizing his time efficiently is an absolute necessity. Competitive junior players would do well to get into the habit of organizing their own time and playing schedules now, while the pressure is still relatively light.

I've talked about pacing matches, and the same principle applies in deciding which and how many tournaments you're going to play each season. You don't need to play every event you can get into: that's a quick way to burn out. Be selective and consistent. Whenever possible, give yourself some time between tournaments to recharge your batteries and to work on any areas of weakness you have discovered during competition. One of the

McEnroe's selective appearances in junior tournaments included the most important 18-and-under team event in the world: the Sunshine Cup, in which he and Larry Gottfried captured the 1976 title for the U.S.

Dick Kassan

juniors I started in the game is David Wells-Roth, a top-ranked fourteen-year-old who is already an old hand at scheduling tournaments. For a junior between the ages of twelve and sixteen, twelve or thirteen tournaments a year is plenty, he believes. Which ones to play depends on how your association sets up its events. In the Eastern Tennis Association there are six Grand Prix events, all of which offer points toward a place in a sectional tournament that decides which players will go to the Nationals. For juniors who do not have a great deal of tournament experience, there are also smaller drawback events. As for Nationals, there are four tournaments for each age group, on different surfaces: the Indoors, Hard Courts, Clay Courts, and the Nationals. There are also a series of international junior events: the Rolex at Port

Washington, the Orange Bowl in Miami, the Grass Courts in Philadelphia, and the Grand Slam junior tournaments, to name a few. The top juniors are chosen for the Junior Davis Cup teams (there is one for 18s and one for 21s, with most pro events awarding wild cards to those players). Junior Davis Cuppers get their travel expenses paid, accommodations, and an allowance each week to cover meals. Sometimes at this level you can also get help from your local association and tournament officials, especially with accommodations.

Once you've worked out which tournaments you're going to play, you need to learn how to organize yourself for the day of the match. Many juniors just turn up and socialize with friends until they're called. That's a waste of energy and a bad habit. Although I have stressed that you should try to have other involvements, in a tournament event all your energies must be channeled to maximum performance. Doing as well as possible during competition should be, if for no other reason, simply a matter of pride. The pros structure their whole day around the match; they

Young McEnroe at the Port Washington Tennis Classic

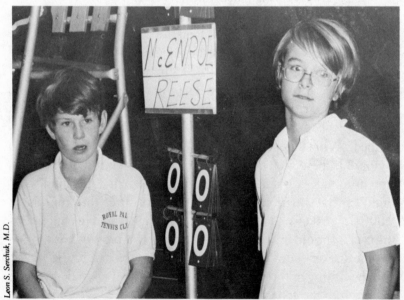

Leon S. Serchuk, M.D.

know when they must practice, when and what they must eat, when they must arrive at the courts. They understand completely the importance of timing. Pros also have the advantage of knowing approximately when they are going to be on court. In the juniors, you generally only know the exact time you're playing if yours is the first match of the day or the last match of the tournament (the finals). This makes good organization all the more important.

The first step is to develop a prematch routine that you follow as often as possible. It is very reassuring to go through a familiar series of actions in a tournament environment, which can seem extremely alien and hostile. Try to figure out roughly the time of your match—it doesn't have to be precise—and then work backward from that time to organize everything you need to do before playing. Say you're going to be on around 3:00 P.M. Forty-five minutes beforehand, at 2:15, you should be in the locker room stretching out, getting changed, psyched, and ready. About three hours before the match (12:00 noon) you should have *finished* eating. Since you should allow about half an hour to eat, you should get to the eating place around 11:30. You need about 30–45 minutes between the end of your practice session and the time you eat, so you should be coming off the court around 11:00. The prematch practice session should ideally be an hour, so that means you should try to be on the court around 10:00 A.M.

As anyone who has ever played a junior tournament knows, no matter how small the draw, they rarely run so smoothly that you can neatly fit in the full prematch routine that I have just described. What happens if the practice courts are all full at ten o'clock? If there aren't any practice courts? If your match doesn't start until 4:00? Or if it is scheduled for nine in the morning? Naturally, as the situation changes so must you alter your routine. A 9:00 start makes practice difficult, although possible, but everything else should be observed. Two important parts of this routine are the locker-room arrival forty-five minutes before the match and the timing of the meal. Those two elements should always be worked into the schedule properly.

During the early rounds of a tournament, the hardest part of the routine (no matter what the event) is getting practice time. If you do happen to get a practice court, you shouldn't just hit around but go on with specific goals. If you don't, at least find a backboard. Warm up each individual shot, get used to your surroundings, and then play a few points. The key to a successful practice session, especially those before a match, is to be positive and competitive. You shouldn't spend time at a tournament drilling on shots that you feel are faulty; this can emphasize your lack of confidence in a technicality and start tipping the mental balance in your opponent's favor before you've even gone on court. You can, and should, practice certain shots and tactics that you think are going to be useful against your opponent. (Wilander, before his final against McEnroe in the Association of Tennis Professionals, or ATP, Championships at Cincinnati in 1983, went out and practiced chipping and coming in to the net because he figured he'd have to come in in order to break up John's aggressive game.) A good tournament practice session would be split up as follows:

- Fifteen minutes of getting a feel for the strokes
- Fifteen minutes of shots/sequences you expect to use in the match
- Thirty minutes of playing points

Note: Try to play points rather than games or sets. You are still competing and working on different strategies.

The part of the tournament in which you can socialize with friends, play video games, or whatever is the time between practicing and eating. It is generally a good idea to try to keep those activities as far away from the match as possible. When you are actually in the locker room for the forty-five minutes immediately preceding the match, try to do the same things in the same order each time: stretching out, changing, and getting ready.

Many young players don't really know what getting and being psyched actually is. They sometimes confuse it with being wild or aggressive. Getting psyched and being psyched has nothing to do with being physically aggressive: you don't need to smash your arms on the lockers or beat your head against the wall. You're a tennis player, not a boxer or a football player. They're getting ready for a war of physical attrition in which they will need to crunch and be crunched. If a tennis player got that pumped up, he'd be fencing balls from the start. In tennis, getting psyched means getting physically relaxed and calm, and focusing all your attention on the match, collecting your energy so that when you need it on the court it will all be there at your fingertips. Being psyched is being absolutely ready.

I always used to find that the worst time was between eating and going to the locker room to get ready. It's a real limbo period during which many players start getting very edgy; what makes it harder is that you can't afford to do anything too hectic, which

McEnroe's alternative to video games during his early junior years

World Tennis

would take your mind off the match and possibly drain valuable energy. A couple of ways to fill this void would be listening to music or reading.

If your prematch routine has been effective, you'll go into the match feeling calm and confident, with that "let's see what you've got" attitude toward your opponent. You won't feel you have to hit winners from the start. You let him set the pace while you stay with him until the first big point. Then you rev up and nail him. The thing to remember is that psyched means absolutely ready— *not* pumped up like a Mr. T.

The other subject that many juniors misunderstand is the five-minute warm-up (recommended time) that you have with your opponent just before starting the match. What should your aim be? Initially, you should just be trying to get used to the court, the surroundings, the weather conditions, and your shots, not worrying about anything else. You are loosening up, so you don't need to blast any balls. Just build up your timing and your feel. Nor do you need to lunge for any wide shots. Gradually, start going for better strokes and running a bit faster for your opponent's shots, and by the end hitting a few stingers and pressing shots. Especially on the overhead, don't go for anything huge and run the risk of mis-hitting the ball; just ease it in while you build up confidence. You should be communicating to your opponent a feeling of supreme confidence, the air of a player who isn't hitting winners yet but certainly can when he wants.

Should you be trying to test the other player out? It is certainly worth checking out the opponent to see what he's got and maybe try him on a couple of wider balls, but if you're holding back your best, there's no reason to assume that he isn't doing the same. So the main focus of your attention should remain on your strokes rather than his. The old adage about winning the warm-up by impressing your opponent with great shots is a fiction. Use the time for grooving that attitude of calm self-confidence, rather than trying to win some make-believe struggle. You don't get any points for winning the warm-up.

When it comes to deciding what to take to a match, just use

your common sense. You should have at least two rackets in reserve (preferably two strung with gut and one with synthetic) in case of bad weather or a series of broken strings. Be responsible enough to take care of your equipment. Check your frames and strings well in advance in case they need replacing or repairing. Always take a couple of extra shirts, and it's also a good idea to have a spare pair of shoes, even extra shoelaces and wristbands. When these are not provided by the tournament, be sure also to bring sawdust, a water jug, and, of course, a towel.

Reminders

- Doing as well as possible during competition should be, if ·for no other reason, simply a matter of pride.
- The key to a successful practice session, especially those before a match, is to be positive and competitive.
- In tennis, getting psyched means getting physically relaxed and calm, and focusing all your attention on the match, collecting your energy so that when you need it on the court it will all be there at your fingertips.
- If your prematch routine has been effective, you'll go into the match feeling calm and confident, with that "let's see what you've got" attitude toward your opponent.

Patrick McEnroe's Commentary

Many kids in the 12s and 14s get too worked up about their results and rankings. You should learn to keep it in perspective. By
the time you're in the 18s, none of those results matters anymore;
I can hardly remember them. I was only ranked in the top thirty
or forty in the 12s and 14s, but that's nothing to worry about.
Some kids get so obsessed with getting a good ranking at the age
of thirteen that they won't play some tournaments in case they
might hurt their ranking. That's stupid. When you're a junior,
your priority has to be the competition and gaining experience,
not what your National 12-and-under ranking is.

At the same time, you don't want to go over the top. You don't
need to play more than ten or twelve tournaments a year. Tennis
shouldn't be dominating your life then, not even when you're
sixteen or seventeen. You should try to get away from tennis,
have other friends outside the sport, and play other games. Tennis should be fun. I certainly still regard tournaments as fun. In
the summer of 1983 I went to Wimbledon, did well in the U.S.
Open as well, and met loads of new people. With the summer
over, I went back to school and played soccer again.

At the beginning of 1983, I was nowhere near the top in the
18s, and I would never have thought that I'd be finishing the
season ranked three in the nation. I wasn't lazy, but there were
players out there who worked harder than I did. I just played a lot
of tournaments and kept on taking them one match at a time. I
realize I have weaknesses; I'm not the quickest player around, so
I'm working on that. But you must also stay sane and keep things
in proportion.

I don't really worry too much about playing professionally. I
don't spend time thinking how close to, or far from, playing
Wimbledon or the rest of the pro circuit I am. In the juniors I
just tried to concentrate on winning matches, on getting to the
top of my age group. In college, I'll try to do the same thing:

Patrick McEnroe, one of the world's top junior players

Michael Cole

focus on becoming a top college player and not worry about getting a world ranking.

The same is true of a lot of the other top 16s and 18s I know in the States. They keep their minds focused on the juniors while they're juniors, on the immediate competition. But some European kids aren't like that. Players like Guy Forget and Stefan Edberg start playing pro events earlier and aim to make it earlier. In the States it's different because college tennis is so good. Where a seventeen-year-old in Europe is already playing the pros in a limited way, over here you can go to college, keep up your standard, and play a few pro events. You don't have to make the choice between tennis and education, which I think is a plus for Americans.

At the same time, there is certainly a growing trend among juniors to try to turn pro after the successes of Borg and Wilander, and now Arias, but I certainly don't feel pressured into trying to make it any earlier than I think is sensible. The fact is, there are only so many guys who are able to make it that young, and they're way ahead of the rest of us. Most kids playing junior events just aren't good enough, at least not yet, so trying to copy those who are is crazy. Sure, the girls are turning pro younger and younger, often with a lot of success, but that's a little different because the physical gap between a teen-age girl and a woman isn't as great as that between a sixteen- and a twenty-year-old man.

So at the moment I'm not really thinking about satellite circuits, computer points, or winning the U.S. Open, whereas a lot of the foreign kids I play are. That's the difference between the two philosophies. Their immediate goal is to make it; mine is to go to school. I'm going to take it one step at a time, see how I do in college, and then, when the time comes, decide whether to play pro or not.

The main thing, I think, is being a strong competitor. I have never felt that I couldn't play against a player because he was bigger or faster. I've just taken it one point at a time, tried to win each match, and let everything else take care of itself. *I don't really care about how great my ranking is, just about winning each match. And you don't have to be ranked three in the nation to win matches.*

14

MAKING IT: HOW TO MAKE IT WHEN TO MAKE IT

When a tennis player talks about "making it," he means getting onto the professional circuit and being good enough to earn a living from playing.

These days young players are making it big earlier and earlier. Andrea Jaeger had won her first million by the time she was seventeen; Kathy Rinaldi was winning matches at Wimbledon at fourteen; Tracy Austin took the U.S. Open at sixteen, and Bonnie Gadusek, who broke her neck doing gymnastics at the age of thirteen, turned to tennis and made $100,000 by the age of nineteen.* Some may say, "True, but in the women's tour, it's easier to make it." That may be so, but even in the men's game, big money and big titles are beginning to go to younger and younger faces. Borg played Davis Cup at fifteen, Wilander won the French Open at seventeen, Jimmy Arias was seeded nine in the 1983 U.S. Open at age seventeen, and Aaron Krickstein, the latest youngster to burst on the scene, reached the quarter-finals of

---

*Bonnie had a cast for six and a half months after breaking her neck in gymnastics, which she was doing to enhance her ballet. She was training for the 1980 Olympics when that accident occurred. Three months out of the hospital, she played in her first tennis tournament.

the U.S. Open in 1983 at the age of sixteen.

Therefore, if you are an ambitious and exceptionally talented junior player, turning pro today isn't a distant dream: it can be just around the corner. However, I believe that the vast majority would do well to concentrate first on their junior careers with an eye on college tennis and its many benefits. With racket companies, clothing manufacturers, and players' agents scouting junior events, looking for future prospects, it can become a real temptation to redirect your goals. Note of caution: be realistic and recognize your capabilities!

Many of today's junior players are already getting a taste of the lives led by the pros. In the States alone there are over two thousand junior tournaments a year, and competing in the Nationals involves commuting throughout the country. A top fourteen-year-old spends most of his school vacations at thirty thousand feet, flying from tournament to tournament. In 1981, the international junior circuit, a proving ground for players such as Lendl and Mandlikova, comprised sixty tournaments in thirty-two countries. Two years later it was eighty-four tournaments in forty-one countries, and it keeps getting bigger all the time.

So the juniors are getting tougher, and some of them are breaking into the circuit early.

The way the world ranking works today actually favors the unknown player looking to make a big break onto the circuit. Look at the way Wilander made it when he won the French Open in 1982.

The French Open had a total of $450,000 in prize money. A tournament gets one star for each $25,000 of prize money, so the French had eighteen stars. It had an additional three stars for having 128 players in the draw (a Grand Slam event) and three more because the combined total ranking of the top twenty players in the tournament was under 450. That made a total of twenty-four stars, which translated into 250 ATP points for the winner.

In addition, Wilander picked up bonus points for individual wins over highly ranked opponents: four points each for his wins over Lendl, Vilas, and Clerc because they were seeded in the first four; three more for beating Gerulaitis, who was seeded in the second four. Because Lendl, Vilas, and Clerc were all ranked in the top eight in the world, Wilander got three more points for beating each player. Finally, he added two more points for the win over Gerulaitis because Vitas was ranked between nine and sixteen. So he got twenty-six bonus points, making 276 points in all, which lifted him to number twelve in the world.

McEnroe had basically the same rapid ascension in 1977, when he played right through the qualifiers at Wimbledon and made the semifinals. (He was, not incidentally, the only qualifier and the youngest male ever to reach the semi's at Wimbledon.) The point is, the system is wide open to newcomers: if the cat can get among the pigeons, he gets really fat. That is not to say it's easy—no match on the tour is easy—but if you're tough and determined, you can get in.

What sometimes happens is that a player will break into the top hundred after one good tournament but then get stuck: for

Carillo-McEnroe team, after winning the French Open mixed doubles in 1977

Michael Cole

Borg during his first Wimbledon match, June 6, 1974

Ed Lacey

months he doesn't make any further dramatic moves upward. After this he loses heart and gradually drops down again. The problem is there are far more points separating the top hundred players from one another than the bottom four hundred, so a good batch of points can catapult you from the bottom of the computer to the top hundred. But to make another big move after that, you have to win far more points. Paradoxically, the higher you are in the rankings, the more difficult it is to move up.

Most juniors think that getting computer points means playing satellite circuits, but that is only partly true. The problem is, there are hundreds of players vying on the ATP satellite circuits, from Borneo to Belgium, fighting for just a handful of points. Five weeks of consistent success on the satellites might bring you, say, twenty-five points, whereas a mere two weeks on a rampage at a major event could take you into the top hundred.* Most players who burst into the pro game and stay in the top twenty don't spend years trailing around the satellites hoping to pick up the odd point. The danger of "satellite strategy" is that your goals could begin to change and you can get stuck there. The key, as Peter Fleming notes, is not to get hung up about getting points. Think only in terms of improving your game, mentally, physically, and technically. Get tougher, and keep exhausting all the competition at your level; everything will fall into place naturally.

Reminders

- Many of today's junior players are already getting a taste of the lives led by the pros.
- The system is wide open to newcomers: if the cat can get among the pigeons, he gets really fat.

---

*Rankings for the men's game in 1984 are issued jointly by ATP and Hewlett-Packard. Some changes have been introduced. Star categories are awarded as follows: one star for each $25,000 increment, up to $150,000 in prize money; one star for each $50,000 increment between $150,000 and $500,000; one star for each $75,000 increment for tournaments with prize money exceeding $500,000. Additional stars are awarded for tournaments with prize money in excess of $150,000 and with draws of 48 and larger: 48 draw equals one extra star; 56 draw, two extra stars; 64 draw, three extra stars; 96 draw, four extra stars; 128 draw, six extra stars. A player gets bonus points by defeating players ranked from 1–150, as follows: players 1–5 equal 30 points; players 6–10 equal 24 points; players 11–15 equal 20 points; players 16–20 equal 16 points; players 21–30 equal 12 points; players 31–50 equal 6 points; players 51–75 equal 3 points; players 76–100 equal 2 points; and 1 bonus point for wins over players ranked 101–150. This means that if you defeat players ranked 1–5 during one tournament you get 150 bonus points. In other words, you really can be famous by Sunday.

Peter Fleming's Commentary

I really didn't decide to give tennis all I had until I was seventeen. I played the Nationals every year from the time I was twelve, but tennis wasn't my whole life then. I played several other sports, too, all of them seriously. I always loved competing and always played to win. I'm not saying that's best for every junior, but it did work for me. Some kids thrive on that total tennis dedication from twelve on, but I suspect there are even more who would do just as well if they tried to lead a more normal teen-age life, playing other sports and making other friends outside of tennis. You can practice being a tough competitor in every sport and at every level. Just because you want to be a tennis player doesn't mean that you can't learn something useful from a tough game of basketball.

Each method has its advantages and disadvantages. If you're a completely dedicated tennis player from the age of twelve on, you will undoubtedly get ahead of players like me technically and in your knowledge of the game. But you may pay for it in other ways because you've only been exposed to one thing: tennis. That could mean that if you do make it, you may not be ready to cope with the pressures and strain of the circuit and may eventually have to drop out. If, however, you do participate seriously in lots of other activities besides tennis, you may end up a more rounded and stable person, but you will have to make up the lost ground in terms of tennis experience. Each of you has to feel which route is best for you, and follow your own temperament and talent.

I had dreams of playing the circuit when I was thirteen and fourteen, but when, at seventeen, I decided to give it my all, my game really came on. I went to the University of Michigan for a year, and then transferred to UCLA, where I became one of the top college players in the country.

As far as actually making the switch to the pro tour, there really isn't any great mystery about it; it just comes as a natural progression. Every kid knows when he's ready to challenge, and only he can know for sure, so it must be his decision, not anyone else's. It has nothing to do with rankings, computer points, or anything else. Each time you have exhausted the available opposition at your level, you move up to the next one, a natural progression, until finally the next level is the circuit.

I don't think you should worry too much about state rankings or even computer points. Especially computer points. It's nice to have them, they can be useful, but they're just a man-made, unnatural system for measuring natural talent and ability. All they do is tell us what has already happened. Better to look forward. Set your goals, whether it's to be one of the two hundred best players in the world or one of the ten best, and then *think about nothing except improving.* Work at your game, build up your knowledge, do everything you can to become the player you want to be, and everything else—the rankings, the computer points—will follow. *Nobody ever failed to become a great player because he didn't have enough computer points.* If you can play, computer points will follow; if you don't have computer points, learn to play better.

If you're going to make it, you've got to love the game—you've got to want to spend every minute you have on the court, finding out more and more about the game. That's why motivation can never come from a coach or your parents; it's got to come from you. And more than just the game, you've got to love the whole business of trying to attain whatever goal you have set for yourself, of dedicating yourself to it. That way the sacrifices and the failures don't put you off; they're just part of a challenge you really love.

15 *TV TENNIS*

The tennis calendar is now so crowded with tournaments, exhibitions, and special events that there are few places in the world where the professional game doesn't venture at some point during the year. Even if you live somewhere the tour never visits, you can still see hours of pro tennis by simply switching on your TV.

The networks no longer show as much of the sport as they once did, but the coverage of the "majors" remains, and with the advent of cable in recent years, you can watch tennis on television quite frequently.

Kids have always had sports heroes and tried to imitate them, but in the past they never had as much opportunity to view them as they do today. But too many juniors (and adults, too) don't know how to get the most from this deluge of media coverage.

In a sense, many armchair athletes watch a sport more intelligently than those who actually play it. Since the armchair athlete has little conception of how it feels to hit a topspin backhand or receive a tough serve, he is less interested in the technical aspects of the game, in how a Yannick Noah or a Wilander is hitting his forehand. Nor are they really interested in playing styles, because they can't really differentiate one from another. A serious junior, however, knows just how it feels to hit a topspin backhand, knows what the difficulties are, and is generally more impressed by the shot-making, by the sheer technical expertise of the pros he sees on TV. Precisely because he can differentiate between various styles and has his own favorites, he can easily get caught up in the less important parts of the game.

Thus on a vital point the armchair athlete's sole concern is generally who will win it, while the ambitious tennis player may easily get caught up in the individual shot-making. It is not wrong to take technical lessons from the pros on TV, but it's inefficient. During play, the camera is usually pulled up and back from the players, making real technique hard to distinguish, while the cosmetic differences of style are highlighted. Most easily viewed—and the only thing that the armchair athlete is able to see—is the way the two players (or the four in doubles) are moving each other about, the strategy and tactics of the match. These are the visible

Connors's sky hook, an unorthodox shot that has won big points for him

signs of the mental struggle that is the most important element in the game. That is what you should be looking for as you watch TV tennis.

Rather than simply thinking, "I really like his forehand," try to establish whether the shot is in fact a real weapon. Is it effective on the big points? Just as you should be thinking about stingers and pressing shots when you're playing a match, you should also be thinking about them when you're watching one. Try to work out what the lights are saying on each point (red? yellow?), whether the pro you're watching is using the Penultimate Play Technique or the Two-Ball Survival Kit. If he's hitting a forehand you really like, test it out by seeing how effective it is on red lights as opposed to green. Does it break down under pressure? If so, why? Try to figure out how the pro sets it up, how he works an opening for it. Try to get inside the pro's head; see if you can gauge how much courage and intelligence he shows on each point, how he is toughing it out. TV tennis is a great way of learning how to think in terms of red, yellow, and green lights, of big points and match pacing. Analyze the game, don't just look at it. If you do see a great shot, ask yourself when it was hit, not necessarily how it was hit. Don't stay on the surface: get into its depth.

If you have a technical weakness in your game—for example, your serve—and you're watching Roscoe Tanner serving, you can learn from it, but you must do so sensibly. Many players will watch him serve, hear the commentators talking about how he hits the ball while it's still going up on the toss, and then stride off to the practice court convinced that they have finally worked out what they must do to transform their shaky serve into a mighty weapon. That, unfortunately, is missing the point. Rather than look at just one player's serve, compare it with others. Try to work out what are the similarities between the two shots rather than the stylistic peculiarities. Lendl, for instance, has a huge serve but an enormous toss. He hits the ball after it has made a relatively long drop. The question is, therefore, what do Tanner's and Lendl's serves have in common? Is one more reliable than the other?

Could either one contribute to your type of game and be used as a model?

Listen critically and intelligently to the commentators. Decide whether their commentary is worthwhile, whether it is relevant to the match or just fluff to fill the time.

Another way to put your TV screen to good use is with a video recorder. Although there is a whole series of teaching tapes on the market now in which top pros and coaches lead you through the various strokes (designed primarily for beginners), the junior player should periodically have someone film him. Being able to see a stroke broken down on a slow-motion camera can give you the "feel" for needed improvement. If you have a stroke that could be improved or one that tends to break down under pressure, video it while you're playing points, or preferably a match. Shots often look fine when you are warming up but start to do very strange things when it's 30–all in the match itself. If you still need to identify the cause of a problem, take a close-up.

To resume, when you watch tennis on TV, try to avoid being drawn into a simple battle of styles; get underneath to the mental game. When it comes to imitating your favorite players, keep your attention on their attitudes under pressure; get the feel of how they think and react on big points rather than slavishly trying to copy their serves or groundstrokes. Just as playing other sports is useful, so is watching other sports. Whether it's a marathon or soccer, get into the mental battle and learn from the toughness and versatility of the winners. A tennis player can learn lessons from a quarterback, a boxer, a goalie, or a pitcher.

Reminders

- Analyze the game, don't just look at it.
- If you do see a great shot, ask yourself when it was hit, not necessarily how it was hit.
- Don't stay on the surface, get into its depth.

John McEnroe's Commentary

When I was a kid, I didn't just look up to tennis players and try to imitate their games. I admired athletes in many sports, and not solely for their athletic ability. I really admired Ali and Namath for a quality I don't think I share with them; that is, they were always really outgoing, always committing themselves in public to accomplishing certain goals and then always coming through. They were never worried about saying they'd win this or do that, and they never ended up looking like idiots because they'd generally go right out and do what they said they would. *They delivered.* On the other hand, guys like Pelé and the Rocket [Rod Laver] were different because they never really said that much. They just kept on performing, kept on winning, without making a fuss about it. They let what they did speak for itself, and that's how I like to think of myself. I don't go around talking about how many titles I've won or how good I am, and I admire that quality in other people.

As far as actually copying what other players are doing, it's similar to what I said about learning the feel for the ball. You can learn the basics of technique from someone else. After the basics, you must concentrate on developing your own natural abilities, which are different from everyone else's. I'm different from Borg; he's different from Connors. It would be crazy for me to try to play like them.

16
EQUIPMENT –
THE NEW WAVE

My aim in this chapter is not to explain the latest advances in racket and footwear design but to outline one or two principles that juniors should know.

As the tennis market has grown and therefore become richer, racket and clothing manufacturers have spent an increasing amount of time and money trying to capture the club and junior market with glossy ads, pro endorsements, and intimidating but enticing catch phrases ("the technology that helped put Challenger into space can now help you win matches"). If you can just remember a few basic points, you can cut through all this hype and make decisions about your equipment based on common sense rather than glamorous ads and pitchmen's lines.

Rackets

As for rackets, the first and most important choice concerns the material: wood, metal, composite.

Wood is the most traditional racket material. Until the early 1970s, almost every player who had ever won a title had done it with a wooden racket. Just by the nature of its design, this type of

124

racket provides control, responsiveness, and feel. You'll also hear that because of the conventional closed throat on most wooden rackets, they are slower through the air and therefore better suited to a baseliner's game than a volleyer's (the fact that McEnroe and other aggressive players made it to the top with conventional wooden rackets suggests that this isn't always true).

Many players began using metal rackets when they were first introduced in the early 1970s. Ideal for fast surfaces, their open-throat design cut down wind resistance, which made them very fast and powerful. Most metal rackets are generally stiff. Although aluminum is much softer than steel, on off-center shots even they transmit a considerable vibration to one's arm.

On the other hand, composites, which combine some of the best characteristics of wood and metal, are also the most expensive rackets. Graphite is the most popular synthetic addition to wooden frames; fiberglass is another favorite. These synthetic additions to the wooden frame give added power to the racket while basically retaining the "feel" of wood alone. They also help dampen the vibration and save the racket arm.

By combining various balances of synthetic additions, manufacturers are able to produce rackets that cover the whole range of options from fine control to maximum power. It is up to you to find which is best suited to your game.

As to head size of the racket, it simply doesn't make sense to me to use a conventional racket nowadays. It's a little like playing today in the NFL with the equipment of yesteryear. There are those who maintain that a beginner learns to hit better strokes if he starts on a conventional racket and moves up later when his shots are grooved, but if he's going to be using mid- and oversize frames for the rest of his playing career, why not start on them young? At Wimbledon in 1983, over 80 percent of the men's draw used larger heads, and the singles finals were divided between an oversize and a midsize. This, coupled with the fact that most racket companies today concentrate their advertising on oversize rackets, would seem to indicate that the days of the conventional head, and of wood, are numbered.

Midsize or oversize, it's really a matter of taste. One drawback of the larger head is that the bigger hitting area can produce a trampoline effect (if you jump onto a four-foot by four-foot trampoline, you don't go as high as if you jump on one that is ten feet by ten feet). This trampolining can make groundstrokes hit under pressure a little difficult to control, though the problem probably won't surface until the late 14s, during the growing spurt. Until then, when the kids are still fairly small, any additional power is a real plus. Providing that the grip and weight are appropriate to his size, a junior starting out should find a mid- or oversize racket to his advantage.

Footwear

Once upon a time it was all canvas tops and rubber soles, but now you can get mesh, leather, and cotton uppers or rubber, polyurethane, and combination soles.

The main advantage of polyurethane is that it is lighter and more durable. The latest designs combine it with rubber or double-density polyurethane and include a softer midsole for shock absorption. As a general rule, the more polyurethane in the shoe, the higher the price.

Single-density polyurethane is pressed tightly together, both to provide the best cushioning possible and to provide enough strength to survive a series of hard beatings. However, it is not as tough as dual-density polyurethane and so isn't considered ideal for cement and other rough surfaces.

Dual-density polyurethane has a softer compound in the midsole for cushioning, and a dense, hard compound on the outside for durability. Some manufacturers' "hard outsole" will be softer than others, so use your fingers to check before buying. Basically, the harder a material feels, the longer it will last, but the less cushioning it will give.

Many of the advances in tennis footwear have come as a result of the breakthroughs in the design of running shoes, reflected in the growing involvement of manufacturers in both markets. However, tennis shoes cannot be built to match their running brothers simply because of the demands of the sport. A tennis player needs support for both the lateral and twisting motions of the game. These motions put different stresses on shoes and feet than does the simple forward motion of running.

With shoes it is largely a matter of finding a brand that fits the particular size and shape of your feet—one brand might be wider or longer than another. Also remember that you should *always* break in a new pair of shoes before playing with them. Twist and loosen them with your fingers, practice in them, walk around in them, but never wear a new pair of shoes in a match. If you do, you may pinch your feet to pieces.

Strings

As for strings, your choice really boils down to gut or nylon. Though gut is more expensive and less durable than nylon, it is better by far for a number of reasons. Gut stands out from its synthetic rivals because of its "instantaneous elasticity." This means less vibration, more power with less effort, and longer contact with the ball, which gives you greater control. Gut is largely made from beef and lamb intestines (there is no such thing as catgut strings, despite the popular myth).

Although there are hundreds of different synthetic strings on the market, each boasting its own special manufacturing technique, they are all made with the same basic material. There is no synthetic "gut," only nylons that have been carefully prepared to make them play better. The cheapest and most common method involves taking one solid filament and braiding strands of nylon around it, then fusing them together. Or, for slightly more power and resilience, braiding the nylon strands over a number of filaments grouped together at the core. Other methods include producing strings that are hollow and then filled with oil. Because oil cannot be compressed, the string maintains its shape under tension and on contact with the ball provides better ball speed and control. Coreless nylon strings are also produced, in which strands of nylon are twisted together to simulate gut, the idea being that they will then adopt some of gut's playing characteristics as well. Finally, there are some nylons to which various substances have been added: carbon, graphite, steel, et cetera. These materials increase the strength of the nylon, but it is a matter of opinion whether they really make the strings play better.

Because gut strings are so sensitive to wet weather, it makes sense to keep one or two rackets strung with nylon. But ideally, whenever you're playing matches you should use gut. As for string tension, it's a matter of personal preference, and until you know your racket well and you have moved into the 14s, stick to the manufacturer's recommended tensions.

When you gaze wonder-struck at the perplexing hordes of designer tennis equipment, remember Beppe Merlo: it is you, not the equipment, that is important.

Reminders

- As to head size of the racket, it simply doesn't make sense to me to use a conventional racket nowadays.
- You should *always* break in a new pair of shoes before playing with them. Twist and loosen them with your fingers, practice in them, walk around in them, but never wear a new pair of shoes in a match.
- Because gut strings are so sensitive to wet weather, it makes sense to keep one or two rackets strung with nylon. But ideally, whenever you're playing matches you should use gut.

John McEnroe's Commentary

In some ways I wish everyone was still using a conventional racket; when that was the case you could more easily distinguish the differences in talent. Still, now that I've switched to a mid-size frame, especially my serve and volleys have improved. I changed mainly because I was having a problem with my shoulder, which was affecting my game. With a wooden racket you have to put a lot more into your swing to get results, and my damaged shoulder made that increasingly hard. On the other hand, with the Dunlop Max 200G, the racket does a lot more of the work and has helped the shoulder.

Mid-, oversize, and composite rackets are the wave of the future, and I'm always willing to do anything that will make me a better player or help me win more matches, even though I still have an affinity for the old wooden rackets. The new rackets, composites and larger heads, are giving players so much power that it has changed the whole game. In fact, tennis is already very different from the way it was even when I first turned pro, and that was only in 1978.

17
PLAYERS AND PARENTS

On the junior circuit the phrase "tennis parent" has emerged almost as a term of abuse. Coaches are frustrated by them, kids moan about them, and spectators laugh about them. The poor parents can't seem to do anything right. The touchiness of the subject indicates how important it actually is. Yet, though everyone seems ready to criticize, not many seem willing to offer any practical advice to the often confused parents about how they should cope with a child obsessed with tennis.

Parents

In a game already filled with so much pressure, why add to it with a bad relationship at home? If a kid has had to fight for everything he's got and has had to learn self-sufficiency too early in life, he may be a tough competitor but will often not be a versatile one. He may fight doggedly but be unable to sit back and analyze, and thus can become easy meat for someone who takes a thinking approach to the game. The fact is, the better the relationship between the player and his parents, the better chance a junior has of making it. No parent can buy or give his child success; a young-

Bill Eppridge

John M. Heller

Whether during competitive pressures or practice sessions, a good laugh is a great tension release.

ster needs his parents' love and support, but, as with the fabled stage mother, too much of a good thing can be dangerous. Remember: tennis should be fun.

Tennis parents' first job is to be clear about their child's goals and to appreciate that they are *his* goals, not the parents'. This said, it is very easy for parents to get so caught up in the child's goals that they make them their own. If parents get too involved with these goals, they tend to build up pressure on the child, whether consciously or unconsciously, and this can be dangerous.

My best advice to parents is to enjoy watching your child compete. This book is meant to teach him how to think in terms of challenges, not of problems, and you must help him by having that same attitude. Never communicate your disappointment to him after a loss or a setback. Instead, sit down and analyze it, as he would do a shift in mental balance during the match. This makes him feel supported and you involved. It also turns any negative feelings of disappointment into practical plans for the future.

"But suppose the kid keeps on making the same mistakes? How can I get him to learn? I *have* to get tougher!"

Wrong. If a junior keeps making the same mistake, it is because he has not yet understood the correction. This means either that you have to explain it better or that he isn't ready to learn it yet. Keep analyzing things with him, and when he's ready to learn, he will. No matter how frustrating you find all this sometimes, only he can win the matches, and the best way you can help is by encouraging and supporting him. Remember, no kid was ever frightened or threatened into the top ten.

"What if his motivation begins to fade? If he's not going out for his runs anymore or is skipping practice, shouldn't I nag him about it?"

Once again the answer is no. You can't be the motivator; only a supporter. If he's going to reach the top or anywhere near, the motivation has to come from him and him alone. If it does begin to slacken, go back to that first priority: tennis should be fun. Millions of kids go out running and go to practice because they love playing the game. It's fun. Often when a kid loses his motivation, it's because the game isn't fun anymore—sometimes because a parent gets too heavy about the game. Involvement and support: two key words always to bear in mind.

"That's all very well, but if I'm spending several thousand dollars a year on a child's tennis expenses, it has become a bit more than just having fun."

Wrong. The fact is, if a young player stops having fun, you can forget having a tennis champ in your family. Besides, no one has to spend that much money. Finance, like better competition, comes as a natural progression. If the child has really exhausted all the available opposition in his area (be it state or region), then the state tennis authorities will make travel funds available, or the rising junior will want and need to go further so badly that he'll find a way: riding with someone who's driving, or lodging with a local tennis family, for example. Once again, a sensibly spent amount of money can make the junior's life easier, but ultimately it's his own attitude that counts, and that, like love, cannot be bought. More important to the junior than the actual writing of checks is a willingness to help and encourage him during these crucial years. Feeling this support will do far more for the child than any amount of money. In fact, spending too much money can actually be counterproductive, by increasing the pressure on the junior to succeed and fostering guilt if there isn't an immediate return on the investment.

Players

If you're a junior and feel you're getting short-changed by your parents, remember that no matter how good or bad you think they are (and no matter how good or bad they actually are), only you can make it. Having the most relaxed, most generous, most supportive parents in the world, with your dad a former Wimbledon champion and your mom a one-time varsity player from Stanford University, can only make it easier, just like a warm shower makes washing your hair easier and more comfortable than a cold one. But being a professional athlete has nothing to do with being comfortable; it is about being committed. That is why Zina Garrison made it, that's why Eddie Dibbs and Manuel Orantes made it. They weren't born into country clubs and private coaching. It wasn't easy, but they wanted it badly and they got it.

Also remember that most kids at some time or other think that their friends have better parents (the grass is always greener on the other side of the fence). The fact is, the perfect parent does not exist. For that matter, neither does the perfect kid. The temptation is sometimes strong to start blaming defeats and disappointments on your parents when in truth you are the only one responsible, the only one who can do something about them.

The best possible way to get your parents to be more behind your tennis is to get them more involved. Many parents only make contact with their children's tennis when they come out to the courts to pick them up after practice, take them to tournaments, or pay their court fees and subscriptions—in other words, when they are always giving. Try to get your parents more involved. Talk about the people you've met and played with. Explain to them how the tournaments work and who the top kids are. Get them interested, get them excited, so that they don't feel your tennis is some private world that takes you away from them, relegating them to the lowly role of banker. If you get your parents on your side, it's worth two points a game. At least.

Players and Parents

A more fashionable but equally sensitive relationship is that between the junior and his coach. Many parents, intimidated by what appears to be the closed world of the game, and persuaded by the example of Borg, Navratilova, Vilas, Kevin Curren, Steve Denton, and many other top pros, have surrendered their kids to the protection of one of a string of revered coaches. Many juniors waste valuable time and energy looking for the right pro. At top

junior tournaments coaches scout the new faces for potential re-
cruits to their traveling junior squads, and the tennis world is full
of who's coaching whom.

The possible benefits of these player/coach relationships are ev-
ident: the wealth of talent springing from Bollettieri's Academy,
Landsdorp's success with Tracy Austin, and most recently the
domination of the women's game by Navratilova. However, there
is the danger that young juniors, who are obviously very impres-
sionable, can become dependent on the strong adult personalities
who are acting as both guardian and coach. They look for their
coach's eye on the big points, come to rely on his companionship
at tournaments, his analysis of their and their opponents' games.
The result could be that the mental toughness is only there when
he's there, and these juniors are not making themselves tournament tough. When the original coach has left the scene, the feeling of dependency remains, and someone else has to take his
place.

For the Austins, the Ariases, the Borgs, and the Bassetts, this
has apparently not been a problem: they were already tough com-
petitors. But for kids with less natural mental resilience and therefore with more to learn, it can be a danger. Surprisingly, Borg's
relationship with Lennart Bergelin has not set a trend for the
coaching business in Sweden. With only 20 percent of the clubs
able to afford full-time pros, coaching is primarily volunteer.
Their system promotes a low-key approach in which the young
Swedes develop responsibility for their own training. In their junior program, one finds groups mixed in age and in ability. Ake
Magnusson, Wilander's trainer, is a schoolteacher and cannot
spend his limited coaching time working simply on technique. In
his program, the importance of developing a positive attitude toward the game is heavily stressed. Roland Hansen, another of
their leading junior trainers, believes that the success of his training program lies in the fact that the kids learn to work by themselves, and that even if he were not there, most of them would do
just fine. The success of the Swedish rising stars demonstrates the
validity of a coaching philosophy that includes the development

of the whole person, not just the technical aspects of tennis.

A good coach, like a good parent, gradually makes himself re-dundant. As the kid matures, grows in confidence and indepen-dence, he begins to make his own decisions and takes responsibility for them. For both parent and coach it can be dif-ficult to let go, but, once again, *only* the youngster can win the matches; everyone else has to sit on the sidelines and enjoy watching him. Some of the juniors I've worked with who are now fourteen and fifteen have already reached this stage. They're flying all over the States playing tournaments, and at most I get to see them and play with them once or twice every other month. We do call one another up to chat about their matches, just as I chat with my friends on the professional circuit about theirs whenever we get the chance. Whether they are fourteen or twenty-four, they are tournament tough.

Reminders

- Tennis should be fun.
- The perfect parent does not exist. For that matter, neither does the perfect kid. The temptation is sometimes strong to start blaming defeats and disappointments on your parents when in truth you are the only one responsible, the only one who can do something about them.
- A good coach, like a good parent, gradually makes himself redundant. As a kid matures, grows in confidence and in-dependence, he begins to make his own decisions and takes responsibility for them.

Accomplishment—the pay-off

Professional Sport

John McEnroe's Commentary

There is already enough pressure on a kid playing competitive tennis, especially if he's got high hopes for himself, so it's crazy for parents to put any more on him. It all comes back to that same point: when you're a junior, there are more important things in life than playing tennis, and if you keep the game in perspective, you can avoid a lot of the problems. It doesn't make sense for a parent to yell at a kid when he loses. It's wrong, and it implies that the game is too important. Part of the problem may be that there is so much money in the game these days, and players are beginning to win it at so much younger ages, that some parents begin to see dollar signs. That's sad, because then the kids are getting pushed aside. As in all sports, most of the kids hoping to turn pro won't do it. Only a few will. It just doesn't make sense for someone to sacrifice his childhood by making the game so important that he can't move because of the pressure. If he doesn't make it, what then? He hasn't got anything left.

The serious junior has to learn how to make his own decisions; he should be around other people, whether older players or coaches, who can advise him. Parents can get too involved. (But, then, so do some coaches.) It's more of a personal preference when it comes to how close you get to a coach. The danger is that the coach can become bigger than the player, almost more important, and the coach's expectations and goals become more important than the junior's. It's a matter of independence. The player always has to be the most important member of the team, not anyone else, no matter who—coach, parent, or manager. Only the player can go out and play the match; so, finally, he is the only one who should count.

The correct role for a parent is one of support. When the junior player has a bad run of matches, try to understand the pressures and his reactions to them and, if you can, discuss any weaknesses or mistakes that you feel his most recent matches have exposed. But do so gently, and make sure that it never stops the game from being fun. After all, that's the only reason anyone starts playing tennis in the first place.

GLOSSARY

Approach shots: Shots usually executed around mid-court "en route" to the net.

Break point: The point in which the server could lose the game.

Carving the point: The process required to win a point through the use of strategically selected shots.

Chipping: Back spin or slice shots.

Choking: The sensation felt when a player is under pressure, causing a metabolic change that affects reflexes and instinctive performance.

Clay court: Literally, the internationally popular red clay material (brick dust). Can also commonly refer to green clay, a comparable synthetic material made of chemical particles that has superior drainage qualities. Both are considered slow playing surfaces.

Dropshots: Low bouncing shots just over the net.

Fast surfaces: Generally, all surfaces other than clay courts, although some synthetic playing surfaces are also manufactured for a slow-bouncing effect.

First volleys: Volleys that follow an approach shot, overhead, or serve.

High-percentage moves: A tactical term for shots selected for their likelihood of success.

Killing stroke: A powerful, winning shot.

Love and love: A scoring term sometimes used instead of 6–0, 6–0.

Low-percentage shots: Shots involving considerable amount of risk and therefore less likely to succeed.

Margin for error: An individually determined distance from boundaries and obstacles on the tennis court, which helps to ensure the success of certain shots.

Match point: A point upon which the fate of the match depends; possibly the last point of a match.

Mental balance: The existing condition of the psychological struggle between opponents. The balance is affected by shifts in psychological advantage and determines the offensive/defensive posture of the players.

Mental groove: A sort of "overdrive state of mind," during which a player is able to perform beyond his normal standards.

Mixing up the pace: Mixing the power of the shots during a point, or from one point to another.

Net game: Volleys and overheads.

Passes and passing shots: Successful shots that go by the opponent at the net.

Penultimate-Play technique: A strategy that utilizes imagery to focus the player's concentration on the execution of "set-ups for winners" as opposed to "going for winners." Designed to help the player develop the point tactically and use the percentages in his favor.

Power game: Aggressive style of play.

Prematch routine: The entire process of preparing oneself for a tournament match; a familiar series of actions used prior to the match, which has the purpose of focusing concentration toward maximum performance.

Pressing shot: An alternative to a passing shot but with a higher likelihood of success.

Psychological advantage: Having the mental balance in one's favor, with the opponent under pressure; the edge one player has over the other. The psychological advantage can shift from one player to the other throughout the match.

Pushing the ball: Keeping the ball in play with defensive shots, either by choice or lack of confidence.

Rally: Exchanges between opponents' groundstrokes.

Service-break: A game that was lost by the server.

Spins and dinks: Tennis slang describing an unpredictable, playful style comprised of various spins and dropshots. This technique is used to tease or cajole the opponent.

Staying back: Playing from the back court and relying solely on groundstrokes during a point.

Stinger: A shot that puts sufficient pressure on the opponent, forcing him to return it defensively.

Trick shots: Unpredictable and unorthodox shots.

Two-Ball survival kit: A strategic technique that is applicable to "losing" situations during a match. Designed to short-circuit the tension produced by big points, its goal is to get the ball safely into play at least twice after a serve or a return of serve.

Two-Selves technique: A technique used to analyze the mental balance of a match, to determine and execute those steps needed to shift or keep that balance in one's favor. An imaginary split of personalities in which the Commentator Self constantly analyzes the overall condition of the match, the crowd, the weather, and the opponent. The other Player Self listens to and follows the Commentator's recommendations.

Under pressure: When the opponent has the psychological advantage; also used to describe a player who is off balance while trying to return a particular shot.

Versatility: The ability to adapt one's game to a variety of circumstances encountered during a match.

Volleys: Shots executed before the ball bounces.